THE JOURNEYMAN PIANO PLAYER
Adventures in Gracious Dining

BOB MILNE

(c) 1992
Robert Milne
Lapeer, Michigan

Copyright 1992 by Robert Milne
Published by Woodland Press
P.O. Box 586
Lapeer, Michigan 48446

No part of this book shall be reproduced, stored in a retrieval system, or transmitted by electronic, mechanical, photocopying, recording or otherwise, without written permission from the publisher.

While every precaution has been taken to protect identities where deemed necessary, the publisher and author assume no damages resulting from the use of information contained within.

DEDICATION

This book is dedicated to everyone who has ever tried to make a living by playing the piano. May God have mercy upon you.

Bob Milne

The author would like to thank the following people for their help in preparing this book:

- Richard Berry - typesetter, photographer & book layout
- Linda Milne - proofreader & cheerleader
- Mike Montgomery - friend & supporter
- WordPerfect Corporation - for ClipArt Images
- All the characters who came through the doors over the years to make this book possible

Cover photo: Woodbridge Tavern, Detroit, Michigan
by Richard Berry, 1992

INTRODUCTION

Mike Montgomery

I've collected player piano rolls for over forty years. I know many others who collect - and spend big bucks on - automatic musical instruments, not just player pianos but orchestrations, robots made in Europe that sound like real orchestras that reproduce the sounds of horns, violins, drums, the whole works.

When I stand far enough back from all this, I marvel at the lengths some people will go to avoid taking piano lessons.

Then I read Bob Milne's draft of this memoir - **THE JOURNEYMAN PIANO PLAYER.** If I stand far enough back from it, I can't help marvelling at the lengths some people will go to in order to avoid getting a normal day job. Like Bob Milne.

I had a normal day job, with Michigan Bell for thirty-three years, which ended in late 1988. But while I also play the piano and have had my share of trying to do the impossible (play recognizable songs) for the impossible (noisy drunks who came to the party to celebrate some birthday or talk rather than SING), I was always able to be more selective about the joints I was willing to play in.

Bob Milne, it would seem, has been willing to perform in just about any gin mill that asked him to because, as the definition of JPP reads, it's nice to eat.

Bob is a wonderful musician and has a unique style because he didn't start out as a piano player. (He started out as a French horn player, then drifted into piano playing because pub owners were more willing to hire a solo pianist than a solo French hornist. It's basic economics.) As a result, he taught himself some of the piano playing tricks, effects, runs and so on that make his act a really fun one to watch as well as to listen to.

I've always felt that watching someone play the piano who in turn is watching the piano keys is the dullest activity there is. When I play, I watch the keys. How else will I know what I'm going to do next? But Bob may watch the keys, or he may look around the room, or (if bored) he may hike his right foot up on the treble part of the keyboard and play by foot. It's really something to see.

The real showstopper (detailed in these pages) is the piano bench pratfall, where he ostensibly falls off the piano bench. (Well, he really

DOES fall off the bench, but like the true stuntman he is, he never gets hurt.) The only casualty when he pulls this stunt is the piano bench itself. It usually ages considerably each time it falls over. The helluvit is, it's usually the same bench the rest of us have to sit on when WE play, and the bench keeps getting wobblier and wobblier. But it's the price we have to pay for having an artist in our midst.

Bob is a writer as well as a piano player. He's already written a couple of books which are still in the manuscript stage (horror story and thriller genre). And now there's this effort - **THE JOURNEYMAN PIANO PLAYER.**

If everybody who's mentioned in these pages buys a copy, the book will be a success. Knowing Bob, however, these people may get free copies - even the ones whose names have been disguised to ward off the lawsuits.

So even if your name is NOT included here, it's important that you have a copy to 1) help defray the printing costs, 2) help enlighten yourself as to what actually happens in this business, and 3) give Bob the idea that we're just as interested in what's behind the scenes as we are in enjoying the haunting strains of some rag he's out there playing. None of these may ever give Milne a normal day job but it may enable him to stay home more often and spin more tales, thus staying off the highways he hates to traverse. (Of course, nobody held a gun to his head to make him move out into the woods, forcing him to drive anywhere from fifty to eighty miles one-way to a job.)

Bob claims that all these stories are true, and I have no reason to doubt any of them. I know personally that SOME of them are true, (like, I was there when Joe barfed on the piano keys and on my shoes and pants). And I suspect that all of these incidents really happened. But there's something about Bob Milne that seems to attract mystery, intrigue, the occult and the weird. Or maybe it's the characters who are attracted by social drinking, and the Journeyman Piano Player just happens to be there at the time.

Whatever the truth, I think you'll agree with me that this is a special chronicle. If every piano player lived this kind of a life on the job and could write it down, the bookstores would be filled with tales like these. So either this stuff doesn't happen to most piano players or the rest of us simply have poor memories.

Maybe if we could get a videotape of Bob falling off the piano bench and then send it to a California agent, Milne could find 1) work as a stunt man in Hollywood or at least 2) new joints to play in out West as well as 3) new customers for his writing. On second thought, let's leave well enough alone. It's probably too late to change him into a more conventional person. We need him to stay just the way he is.

Bob made an LP a few years ago and it's good, but possibly out of print by now. If you don't have it, you should. Ask him about it next time you see him. 'Cause really, the moral of all this is simply this:

Support Live Music. Someone without a conventional day job needs to eat tomorrow!

Mike Montgomery

Mike Montgomery

August, 1992

Editor's note:

Mike Montgomery is a world-renowned ragtime historian, piano roll and sheet music collector. We are both pleased and honored to have this introduction written by Mr. Montgomery.

AUTHOR'S PREFACE

The piano has always been something to have fun with to me. As far back as my memory goes, I have known how to play one. This is because when I would hear a piano playing, I knew what notes were coming out of it and in what order. (*"Oh, listen to that; the opening to Beethoven's Emperor Concerto is nothing more than a huge E-flat arpeggio. Isn't that beautiful the way he does that?"*)

I would discover little things on the keyboard for myself, such as the way chords are formed, or the only difference between playing in C or playing in D is to move everything up two hammers. Yes, I said two 'hammers.' As a kid, I would look inside my parents old upright piano and see that two hammers equaled what musicians now call two 'half tones,' but they looked more like hammers to me back then.

I knew, from everything I'd heard played, that all music rotated around three basic chords; C, F, and G. I referred to them as my '1, 2, and 3' chords. And since all music, in the key of C, ended on a C chord, I knew that it would arrive back at C by either the mighty G-C cadence or the more etherial F-C sound, which I heard in church whenever they sang 'Amen.' The same sounds were true if the congregation was singing in E-flat, F, or any other key, and the only difference to me was that it was either higher or lower than C. My ears told me exactly what notes they were singing, and the number of hammers between those notes were the same regardless of the key .

Chords other than my little '1, 2, and 3' chords were classified as to texture. An occasional 'e' or 'a' minor chord sprinkled among the melodies was a way of softening up the usual three chords of each tune, and the less-often heard chords, such as D major or F-sharp were colorful flavoring tactics that were like the difference between swimming above or under water.

Yes, pianos were fun. I couldn't take them seriously and resisted my mother's forced piano lessons in the fifth grade, but I do remember playing a recital for the piano teacher in which I played a Schubert favorite in major rather than the written minor because I thought it sounded better. Soon afterward, I was allowed to quit and take up the French horn.

I went to the Eastman School of Music with the horn, and it was there that I learned they had all kinds of different little numbers for my '1, 2, and 3' chords. Now they were to become I, IV, and V chords. Chords in-between had small case numberings, such as ii and iii chords. There were augmented and diminished chords, ninth and thirteenth chords. All of these were already categorized by me in a simplistic way that probably wouldn't stand up to scrutiny, but I'd done it anyway. For instance, an augmented chord was simply a chord 'trying to cave into itself.' (The sound of a C augmented resolving to C gave rise to that description.) A ninth chord was simply a C chord with a D in it (I called them 'side notes'), and a minor chord was really the same as a major chord upside-down. (By looking at the hammers, a major chord has three hammers between the first and second notes, two hammers between the second and third notes. Reverse this and you have a minor chord.) These were the fun little discoveries of a kid learning the working mechanisms to the make-up of chords and harmonies.

So, pianos were fun. Why would anyone want to 'learn' how to play them? I learned the English language by hearing it from birth, so what was so hard about hearing what pianos and orchestras had to say? Can't everyone else hear them, too? What's the big deal here?

The horn took me through about nine years of bliss. By now I was quite used to rehearsals and concerts. I'd been playing horn in the Michigan Youth Orchestra, the Pontiac Symphony, the Interlochen Arts Academy, and several other Michigan orchestras for about three years, and now the music was fantastic! Here were all my little chords, along with a whole host of other 'side notes' dreamed up by masters, and I was right there in the middle of huge, moving masses of musicians making it come alive! The way the music moved, wove among itself, ran up and down the scales, or simply stood alone to wail plaintively haunted me through and through, and I lived for the rehearsals and concerts.

Then, when I got to Eastman, came the myriad of college orchestras that I, as a performance major, was assigned to. Nothing more could be achieved in life, I thought. There were orchestras every day, concerts every week, and musicians of the highest calibre and understanding to mingle with. But then, incredibly, I was asked by my teacher, Verne Reynolds, to play assistant first horn to him in the Rochester Philharmonic. This had to be heaven, and they were actually paying me to do this.

When we'd go out on the stage for a concert, I always tried to hide the little smirk on my face. I knew, from sitting in the rehearsals, that the audience was going to feel and become excited by the slow, unravelling tension as Johannes Brahms unwound his second symphony for them, and I couldn't wait to share it with them. (No, of course Brahms wasn't the conductor. But these guys come alive with an awesome presence when you're sitting in the middle of their music. You can actually see the way they thought!) And when the thunderous applause was over, we'd all go somewhere to sit and relax. Usually, we'd find a piano there, and many times I'd go over and fool around with some of the tunes we'd all just finished playing on the stage.

I always watched people's reactions as I would do this. I'd look at them, rather than the keys, because I wanted to hear what everyone else was hearing, not what I THOUGHT or WANTED to hear as I stared at the keys in front of me. I could see, from looking at people, what they liked and what they didn't particularly like. Of course, I always tried to play what they liked, so I was always watching them.

Thus, I became an observer. I played the piano for fun and for an easy way to make money, even doubting sometimes that it was proper to accept cash for something so ridiculously simple. During long, boring jobs that would go on for years, I would make up things to keep myself interested, at the same time trying to improve my abilities on the keyboard. I have always told myself 'If you can think it, you can do it,' so (not having a piano to practice on until I was ten years into the business) I made up things to challenge myself with as I drove in my car. I pretended I could hear one hand playing in 'three' while the other was in 'four,' and then I'd drum my fingers on the seat accordingly to 'polish the wires between my brain and the keyboard.' It's one thing to know what you're trying to do, but your fingers have to respond to your brain waves.

I would listen, in my mind, to what I wanted to hear come from the piano, and then I'd try to recreate it that night at wherever it was I was playing. Sometimes, while playing, I'd pretend I was sitting in a balcony somewhere out in back of me. From this vantage point, I could see 'me' at the piano, and now relax and listen to anything I wanted to hear. I'd sit up there and listen to myself, and it made the playing even more enjoyable. I would anticipate what 'the piano player' was going to do next, and I'd either nod my head to the fulfillment of what I expected to hear, or smile as the music suddenly took a turn that tricked me.

And so began the Journeyman Piano Player, over thirty years ago. I've played in everything from concert halls and mansions to supper clubs and skid-row dives. Why? Because it's fun. If I can make a stevedore smile as he stands in a riverfront saloon, how can that be any different from the people who jumped from their seats following Brahms? If a melancholy rag brings a tear to someone's eye, how can that differ from a love-torn clown singing 'Ridi, Pagliaccho' on the opera hall stage?

In preparing this book of anecdotes, I have found that some people simply can't believe that this stuff really happened. Well, it did. All of it. In each case, I know of other people who witnessed these events other than myself. The incredible 'Night of the Green Goddess' was witnessed by people who I can pick up the phone and call right now, and their memories of it are just as vivid today as they were back in 1974 when it happened. I haven't had to embellish this book in any way. In fact, other professional pianists who have been through incidents similar to these tell me the following:
"I know these strories are true, Bob. You couldn't make up stuff like this if you had to."

But before we start with the stories, let me share one other interesting side note that concerns when we were readying this book for press, and the word was getting out that various clubs, bars, people, and restaurants were being dug up from the past and put into print. Certain club owners began calling me, and their conversations, always filled with apprehension, would be similar to this:
"Hi, Bob?"
"Yes."
"I understand you've written a book."
"Yes, I have."
"Well, uh, would you mind telling me - JUST WHAT STORIES ARE YOU PRINTING ABOUT MY PLACE?"
Individuals had similar reactions. One particular character (who grew out of the past to become a respected citizen) was reminded of an incident from bygone years. He had this to say, after a moment of nervous silence:
"Uh, Bob; I, uh, I certainly hope you're not using our real names in this thing. You're not, are you?"
When Richard Berry and myself were taking photographs to go in this book, other nervous reactions took place. At one saloon, we found the manager and employees so concerned that we were either from the

IRS, the city auditor's office, or the Friend of the Court that they decided to test our credentials before allowing us to take pictures. I was forced to play the Maple Leaf Rag on their delapidated piano to prove that we were musicians, not moles. After a moment, they broke into smiles and allowed us to proceed. We were given complimentary Cokes for our trouble.

And one final, albeit unbelievable, footnote went into the preparation of this book. As Richard and myself searched the riverfront section of Detroit for a suitable street shot, we found an old brick street among the warehouses and small bars, the Detroit Renaissance Center towering in the background. We began setting up the tripod and attaching the camera to it. As Richard was sighting the camera, some fat slob dressed in a tee shirt and bermuda shorts came boogying out of a bar, half-way down the block. He now started striking poses for us, balancing on one foot for a profile or doing a couple of jumping jacks in the middle of the street.

Richard looked over the camera quickly, not sure he understood what was going on through the sighting mechanism, and now as he looked back to finish adjusting the focus, the character bent over, dropped his shorts, and (to use the vernacular) 'mooned us.' Then he went boogying and shuffling back inside the bar, waving his hand in the air as if he'd lifted his straw boater for us.

As you can see, this book could go on and on, never reaching completion because of the idiotic things that continually happen to journeymen, this one literally coming out of the woodwork in the middle of the afternoon.

So have fun with the stories, poems, and anecdotes in these pages. Be a Journeyman for a while. You'll find, however, that in some of these tales the names have been changed to protect the liable, but maybe they'll remind you of someone or something that's happened along the way. And maybe, next time I see you, we can exchange a few more yarns. Until then, good luck and keep syncopating.

Bob Milne
The Journeyman Piano Player

Movin' On

Photo by Charlie Rasch, 1981

DEFINITION:

JOURNEYMAN PIANO PLAYER: (noun)

Anyone who will drive anywhere today
to play any piano tonight
so he can eat someplace tomorrow

Dakota Inn Rathskeller
Photo by Richard Berry, 1992

DITMAR

The Dakota Inn Rathskeller is a German beer hall that opened in Detroit on the first day prohibition was repealed back in 1933. I began playing piano there in 1964, shortly after leaving the Baltimore Symphony where I was a French horn player during a summer season. Before that, I was at the Eastman School of Music for four years, and had the honor of playing, in the Rochester Philharmonic, assistant first horn to one of the greatest horn players that ever lived, my teacher Verne Reynolds.

The horn is a beautiful instrument, and I have always felt that I've been biding my time until I got another one and started playing with another orchestra. In the meantime, however, I've been playing the piano in such places as the Dakota Inn on and off ever since leaving Baltimore.

The piano at the Dakota (often called the Rathskeller, also) is an upright that sits on a small stage along one wall where the piano player can see most of the place and everyone coming in the door. In the mid 1960's we had a rather colorful character that made frequent appearances there. His name was Ditmar, and he would clearly define for me, an apprentice Journeyman, the differences between the concert halls and beer halls.

Ditmar, with his heavy accent, was German through and through. He always came by himself and every time I saw him grace the doorway I cringed, knowing what was going to happen. Ditmar liked to drink, and he wanted every one in the place to drink with him.

"Come, Bawb; you vill drink Schteinhager mit me, ya?"

Ditmar would stand at the bar slamming down shots of Steinhager and chasing them with beers until no one could understand what kept him standing. In fact, those around him wouldn't be standing. He always dragged someone, either the employees or some unsuspecting customer, into these unbelievable binges until people were actually lying passed out on the benches. Yet Ditmar drank on.

"HA! Schteinhager eese gute, ya? Let's drink!"

The owners didn't know how to handle this at the time. Ditmar spent a lot of money in the place, the public awareness of intoxication wasn't as high as it is today, and the scenes just had to be endured for several years. Finally, though, we couldn't take it any more. There were too many cases of employees not being able to drive their cars home after an appearance by Ditmar, too many hangovers, too many dry-heaves, too many D.T.'s, and on and on. We'd had it and something had to be done. This time, the owners agreed.

Ditmar came back again the next weekend, as we knew he would, only this time none of us would drink with him. We had convenient excuses, and we also shied the customers away. So Ditmar steamed them down standing at the bar alone:

"HA! I like deese place! Ditmar - he can feel like a MAN here!"

'Crash! Bang!' The sound of empty shot glasses hitting the bar pierced through the overall din.

"Come, Bawb. You must drink mit Ditmar!"

"No," I explained. "I don't feel good tonight."

"NONSENSE, Bawb! Schteinhager make you feel gute, like ME! Ditmar, he vill buy you vun! He vill buy you TWO!"

"Uh, no thanks, Ditmar. Excuse me, please. I have to play the piano."

And so went the night. Even as I played all the sing-a-long favorites to a packed house, I could hear him around the corner some fifty feet away becoming roaring drunk as the night went on:

"Eeee - Yahhh! Bartender! Bring beer! Bring gute German beer for Ditmar! I am thirsty tonight! Wha-haaa!"

Finally, closing hour was drawing nigh. Ditmar was screaming and yelling and, in a catastrophic misjudgment of timing, it was then that the owner decided to tell him that this could not go on.

"VHAT? VHAT ARE YOU TELLING ME? EESE NOT DITMAR VELCOME TO DRINK IN DEESE PLACE? VHAT DA HELL EESE RONG MIT YOU, HERR OWNER?!"

An incredible tirade followed, during which Ditmar came shrieking around the corner beating his fists on the wooden tables - (thump, thump!)

"I HATE DEESE PLACE! I HATE ALL OF YOU! YOU PEACE ME OFF MIT DEESE BULL SHEET! DITMAR CAN DRINK ANYWHERE, AND HE DOES NOT NEED DEESE FOCKING DUMP YOU CALL A BAR!"

He stormed out the door, wild-eyed, waving his fists in the air, and screaming obscenities at us. The slamming door shook the whole room, and we did not see Ditmar again for about six months. Finally one night, I looked up from the piano to see that he'd returned. Of course, I cringed again, but this time he was quite different:

"Bawb," he said rather meekly, looking up the stairs at me. "Vhen *you take a break, I must talk to you."*

I agreed, and found him hiding in a corner a little while later. He sat at a table away from everyone else with a cup of coffee.

"Bawb," he began. *"Ditmar eese very confused. Do you remember a night six months ago vhen I vas in here?"*

I told him I did.

"Bawb," he continued. *"Please tell me; vhat did I do?"*

Not wanting to embarrass him, I tried to politely explain that he'd gotten drunk and stormed out of the place.

"Bawb," he went on. *"Vas anyone mit me? Vas I alone?"*

I informed him that he was alone. Now Ditmar stopped talking and looked around the room with furtive, almost scared glances. I realized that if he couldn't remember what had happened that night, then he couldn't remember that he had also been told to cool his act either. So I tried to figure out just what he could remember:

"Ditmar, you do remember coming here, don't you?"

"Ya."

"And do you remember leaving?"

"Nein," he replied.

"Nein?" I echoed, curiously.

"Nein," he repeated, and then followed with this unbelievable statement:

"All I remember is dat de next day, vhen I voke up, Ditmar vas in hotel in New Orleans."

"WHAT?" I blurted in amazement. He turned and looked at me:

"Yes, my friend," he said in dead seriousness. *"Vhen I voke up, Ditmar vas in some rat-dump hotel in New Orleans. I don't know how I got there, or vhere I vas before dat."*

I was too stunned to know what to say. I tried figuring out how he presumedly made it fifty miles to the airport, how his rage could have continued to the point where he boarded an airplane out of town, how he could have travelled all that distance, managed to find a hotel in New Orleans, checked into it, and awoke the next day not knowing where he was or how he'd got there, how he got back, where was his car...

Ditmar eventually declared himself an alcoholic and never drank again. This, undoubtedly, is one of the horror stories that led to his realization. Recovered alcoholics can all tell horror stories, and this particular one is among the most bizarre I've ever heard.

WHAT IS A MUSICIAN?

circa 1976

Does...
A musician earn a living
Making notes upon a horn?
Are they cultured, then, and learn-ed
Or is subtle how they're born?

If some are better, some are worse,
And who are we to say
That a man who blew his heart out
Wasn't good enough to play?

Do they sing? Or strum? Or think in terms
That set them off, apart?
Produce the rot the public buys,
Or too good to ever start?

Possess a sense of beauty
That is quite uniquely his?
Ah! The answer to the question goes...
A musician simply - 'is.'

THE LAST OF THE GREAT CON MEN

Joe was an idiot. We all had to contend with him around the Rathskeller during the mid-sixties. From the small stage where the upright piano sat, I could see everyone who came through the doors, and every time I saw this guy's beady eyes, round wire glasses, and demented smirk come in, something about the frivolity went out.

He wasn't retarded in the sense that he was learning impaired. Oh, no. Joe was a little jerk who could first pass himself off as a junior executive type, and then fleece the place for everything he could get his hands on before they found out just what it was that they'd let through the door. The demented smirk meant that he was scheming even as you looked at him. And although he tried hard to be 'one of the guys,' no one wanted anything to do with him.

Unfortunately for Joe, but fortunately for everyone else, more sophisticated con men have existed. His methods would have made good material in Woody Allen's movie about a bozo thief, 'Take The Money and Run.' The scene where Woody burglarizes gumball machines, takes his date out on the town, then tips the maitre d' with a handful of pennies comes to mind. Joe even looked a little bit like Woody. (No offense, Woody; no offense. It's can't be helped.)

Over the years of playing at the Rathskeller, the Journeyman had to listen to many tales of inept woe from Joe. He would come in the door, get a beer from the bar, be told to leave by every table he tried to sit down at, and then eventually plunk himself down on the piano bench next to me. Even Alice, who used to dance on the table tops, told him to buzz off and leave her alone. So, once again, here was Joe:

"Hi, Bob."
"Mmm."
"How are you tonight?"
"Mmm."

It was during this period of time that I began smoking cigars while playing the piano. A cigar creates not only an ungodly stench, hopefully driving away someone like Joe, but it also allows you to pretend you can't talk with a cigar in your mouth. The monologue continued:

"I'm having a hard time with that old lady's garage I'm putting a new roof on."

"Mmm."

"The nails won't hold the shingles down. They keep coming out."

"Puff - puff; Mmm?"

"Yeah. I hammer four nails into each shingle. When I get done, the whole shingle will lift right up, nails and all."

Silence. I recognize rubbish when I hear it. Then:

"Let me tell you what I did. First I removed the old shingles and the rotten wood under them. I took it right down to the rafters."

"Mmm."

"Then I recovered the roof with four-by-eight sheets of styrofoam."

"MMMM!" (Gag! Hack-hack). "WHAT?"

Joe looked at me indignantly now to say:

"I HAD to use styrofoam, Bob! I only charged her two hundred dollars for the whole job, so I couldn't afford to buy plywood! Anyways, there was this whole pile of styrofoam that I stole from a construction site the night before! But I can't get the f'ing shingles to stick in it...!"

Joe liked to chugg beer. It made him feel important. Maybe Ditmar was one of his heroes. Anyway, one night he'd chugged about six of them and was sitting once again on the piano bench, but fortunately the Journeyman wasn't present this time. Mike Montgomery, the world-renowned ragtime historian, piano roll collector, and perennial Friday night pianist at the Rathskeller, was unfortunate enough to take the brunt of this one.

Joe was laughing and yukking it up. He hoisted another stein, downed it, then bent over and ralphed all over the keys. Mike's fingers went straight up as the flow cascaded across the keyboard and down to the floor. Montgomery leaped from the keys and fled to the basement to hose off his shoes, leaving Joe to explain to the owners that he'd puked the piano. And now Mike, himself a Journeyman, then actually waited for them to wash, scrub, and Clorox the piano in the full presence of the gracious diners that evening. Once done, he incredibly returned and finished the night at the keys without the benefit of rubber gloves. I can't imagine what those eating bratwurst sandwiches thought about the entertainment that night. And if the galloping gourmet had been present, he'd have galloped right out the door, no doubt.

Joe finally got a job selling office equipment. It came as no surprise to us that he suddenly had sample equipment for sale in the Rathskeller at ridiculously low prices. We knew how he operated. Finally, we got word that his employers had called for a State Police investigation as to why their warehouse didn't have any equipment left to sell. It didn't take the cops long. They caught Joe wrenching open a window at two o'clock in the morning. We heard that he told jokes as they were taking him away:

"Oh, geez, fellas; I work here."

Then we received word that the judge had had it with Joe. He sentenced him to something like five years in Jackson State Prison.

It was about a month later when we received a post card at the Rathskeller. I was playing ragtime on this warm summer's eve, and one of the regular customers got up from his table to show me what had arrived in the day's mail. It was addressed to the Rathskeller and 'All The Guys,' and showed a picture of a humongous walled building with guard towers and razor wire all over the place. It was postmarked Jackson, Michigan, and the message began:

"Hi guys! Arrived safely..."

We never saw Joe again.

State Prison, Jackson, Michigan
Photo courtesy of Ella Sharp Museum, Jackson, Michigan

BE SURE TO USE THE CORRECT FINGERING...

Young music students always think that they're preparing themselves for either Carnegie Hall or the London Ritz when they practice scales and sonatinas. Indeed, anyone who can walk into a saloon, sit down and rip off Chopin's 23rd etude (the Winter Wind), then nonchalantly pick up the menu and order dinner is going to be asked if they want a job playing the piano. After they accept the job, however, they're going to find that playing the piano is only a small part of what's required to be a Journeyman. The following two examples come from elegant establishments, and not much short of experience is going to prepare anyone for stuff like this.

In the early 1980's, I received a call from a friend who worked for a large corporation. He wanted to know if I'd play at a company function for him, to be held at the Holly Hotel. I explained that I was already tied up on that particular night, so he countered by mentioning a huge amount of money that was available for this job. I immediately agreed to alter my plans for him.

The Holly Hotel, in Holly, Michigan, is a turn of the century hotel with quaint dining rooms, polished wood walls, the customary narrow staircases and hallways, and plenty of history. It was the scene of one of Carrie Nation's axe-wielding, demon-rum demonstrations back in the early part of the century. Carrie was down on alcohol, and went to great lengths to rail against anyplace that would dare serve it. She axed the bar in the Holly Hotel.

Anyway, with plenty of decades between me and her, I arrived an hour early for the job to mingle with the guests as they arrived. (Music students should note that 'Mingling 101' is not a course you'll find offered on the curriculum, but it's one you'd better learn if you want to be in this business. When I was in music school, we referred to it not as 'mingling' but as 'mongering.') I learned that the meeting would take place in one of the upstairs rooms, so I wandered up the narrow stairs to check out the piano. You guessed it. There was no piano. Worse, the hotel didn't even own a piano.

So now the problem was this: I'd already hired a sub for my regular job, and if no one played the piano for the corporation function at the Holly, no one was going to get paid, either. Therefore, I mentioned the problem to the people most likely to help, the waitresses.

"I have a spinet at home," said one. *"If you can get it over here, you're welcome to use it. I don't know how good it's in tune."*

Of course, I didn't care if it was in tune at all, as long as enough notes worked to slide through the gig. And now a busboy was adding:

"I've got a pickup truck. If the boss'll let me loose for a few minutes..."

The busboy grabbed a few of his friends, and fifteen minutes later they were back, with piano. Now both they and myself (tux jacket on the rack, momentarily), resembled something from a Laurel and Hardy movie as we frantically pulled it out of the pickup, trundled it through the dining room as diners paused in mid-bite, then furiously shoved the thing up the narrow stairs and into the meeting room. A fast table cloth across the back disguised some rather gross appearing blemishes, and a quick key-check showed that most of the out-of-tune notes did indeed work.

A fast shirt change in the hotel lavatory was next. The sweat worked up from moving the piano had to be eliminated, and a quick trip to my car for the travelling bag and spare shirt was followed by a sink bath and wash-down. Time had become short, and the sound of car doors outside heralded the arrival of a large group, undoubtedly the corporation. After a record setting tour de force with Right Guard, it was on to the piano.

When the company guests entered the hotel, the gentle, relaxing strains of ragtime could be heard wafting down the stairs. Only an experienced ear would note that the tunes were all single note melodies, or harmonies well spaced out from each other. When playing an out-of-tune piano, it is disastrous to push down notes which are close to each other because the piano will sound like mud. I smiled to each of the guests as they came through the door as if nothing had happened and rose to greet my friend when he entered:

"Why, Tony; how nice to see you! This place is gorgeous, and thank you for asking me. The piano? Oh, it's excellent! Don't you think it has a nice tone? Now, just look at the lovely view from this window. You're so thoughtful to call me for this..."

Another incident that most music students don't anticipate is the sudden change from the predictable to the unpredictable. Consider the following:

I was asked to play for another corporation function, this time at a fashionable hotel in the suburbs. They had a grand piano in the lounge and a seldom used spinet in the aisleways back by the kitchen. At this particular function, the hotel busboys shoved the spinet out into a ballroom for the meeting. It was filthy, so I had to wipe it down with a cloth before the guests arrived. I also removed the bottom board to let more sound out. Catering managers scowled at me from the sidelines. They'd be scowling more before this was over.

When the guests arrived, some guy with an attitude problem told me to turn the piano around so I was facing away from the tables. I did. Then he told me to sit there while he went through his stiff opening speech. Once again, I did.

"Welcome, welcome, blah...blah..."

He droned on for about ten minutes as I sat silently awaiting his command to start. Finally:

"So now, relax, enjoy yourselves, and listen to, uh, Mr., ur, the piano player."

I ignored all that and began playing the first number, but then the unexpected happened. Suddenly, dark little forms were running all over the floor. They were mice. The piano had turned into a mouse nest as it sat in disuse near the kitchen and now, scared out of their wits by the sudden sound, the things were scurrying all over the place as ladies shrieked and jumped up on chairs.

I did the only thing I could think of. I played Hickory Dickory Dock and kept a straight face, to match that of the bimbo in charge as he sat watching rodents charging back and forth on the rug.

IT JUST DOESN'T MATTER

It was a crisp fall late-afternoon in downtown Detroit. The city had been filled with all kinds of outside publicity surrounding some sensational murders, and the Journeyman piano player was playing in a riverfront saloon as ore freighters honked and howled seemingly in the front door and out the back, churning from port to port.

The Woodbridge Tavern is not a yuppie replica of a 1920's rum-runner's joint. It is the real thing, and everything within is loaded with history. Waitresses ran across an authentic plank floor as they carried food and drink to an eclectic array of customers, and the Journeyman Piano Player played ragtime as the moose head on the wall kept tabs on the crowd behind him.

As Scott Joplin's famous 'Maple Leaf Rag' drew to a close, I was becoming aware that some customers had been gently thumping their beer bottles on the tables to the rhythm. Closer scrutiny revealed about thirty men sitting at tables, all watching as I re-lit my cigar between tunes. Strangely, though, these characters continued drumming their beer bottles on the table as they seemed to be mumbling something in unison:

'Brump - brump- brump' -(pause)- 'brump - brump - brump.'

"Too weird," thought I, and went into a rendition of 'Charmaine.'

Upon completion, I noticed the men were still thumping their bottles and mumbling some chant, not to the rhythm of 'Charmaine,' however, but in the same cadence they had been mumbling earlier:

'Brump - brump - brump' -(pause)- 'brump - brump - brump.'

A glance, a puff of cigar smoke, and the Journeyman Piano Player quickly started playing something else. Thinking that the foolishness could be erased with a thundering boogie, I worked it up to room-shaking intensity before drawing to a close. Applause came from all over, but when the applause died down - THEY WERE STILL AT IT!

'Brump - brump- brump' -(pause)- 'brump - brump - brump.'

At this point, no longer able to ignore these guys, I slid to the end of the bench and leaned closer, trying to hear what it was they were mumbling. In return, they started mumbling louder for the rest of the place to hear as well. Their words came softly at first:

"...It just doesn't matter; it just doesn't matter..."

As the rest of us traded glances, no one knowing what to think, they began to chant louder and louder:

"IT JUST DOESN'T MATTER; IT JUST DOESN'T MATTER..."

And now, finally, one of them was jumping up in their midst. He was about fifty years old, fully bearded, balding, and very respectable looking. I couldn't imagine what he was going to do. Then, in the midst of the chanting, he started waving his arms and screaming at the top of his lungs:

"Here we are - the United Press International - the greatest photographic institution in the world! We go into wars, murders, crime scenes, and riots! We are shot at, spit on, kicked in the groin, and defiled by all we make contact with in pursuit of the finest photographic coverage possible!"

A rumrunner's stopover during Prohibition, the Woodbridge Tavern still caters to Detroit's elite
Photo by Richard Berry, 1992

"We crawl on our guts through mud...!"
(He paused while they chanted...)

"We drench in the rain for hours...!"
(Another pause for chanting)

"We accept shitty pay from our boss...!"
('...it just doesn't matter; it just doesn't matter...')

And now he bellowed out for all he was worth:
"And what kind of recognition do we get for all of this? Well, I'll tell you, ladies and gentlemen; we could fall into the river on location for all anyone gives a damn, because..."
They all came together, thumping and yelling the final chorus that could be heard all the way out in the street:
"IT JUST DOESN'T MATTER! IT JUST DOESN'T MATTER!"
Finished, he sat down to wild applause as the chanting and bottle-thumping finally ended.

I have thought many times, during the years that passed, that this piece of wisdom could be used to avoid more ulcers, heart-attacks, and nervous breakdowns than all that could be learned from any number of psychiatrists. This was free, too. On top of that, it even drowned out the boat-horns for a minute.

**The Sweet Violets Ragtime Band
at the Dakota Inn**
Photo courtesy of a special fan, 1991

THE SWEET VIOLETS RAGTIME BAND

The Sweet Violets Ragtime Band was scheduled to play a concert. When asked for publicity biographies by a local publication, the following was submitted. It was consequently printed and distributed.

WALT GOWER: Clarinet:

Noted for incessant off-the-wall comments. Rumored to have a day job, he refuses to divulge what it is. Quote: *"Ya' can't beat Jelly at his own game!"*

NATE PANICACCI: Trumpet:

Always eager to please, Mr. Panicacci is now wanted in three states and sixteen counties for honoring customer requests to hear INDIANA in the worst way.

TED HARLEY: String bass:

Only member of the band fortunate enough to have an instrument big enough to hide behind when the pie and garbage throwing erupts.

DAN PETRELLA: Banjo:

An assistant Wayne County prosecutor, Mr. Petrella has been successful thus far in warding off the mass arrest of the band by outraged patrons and furious bar owners.

JOHN ANDERSON: Trombone:

From London, Ontario; Citing humanitarian reasons, Mr. Anderson has offered the band asylum in Canada over the Ragminister General's most virulent objections.

BOB MILNE: piano:

Mr. Milne still contends that the world is flat, like all the pianos he has to play on. Sharp, eh?

THE ORCHESTRA DAYS

On the way to becoming a Journeyman Piano Player, I was first a French horn player at the Eastman School of Music. A few things stick in my memory from the orchestra days, and these stories are worth retelling also.

The first one, actually two, involve Tchaikovsky's celebrated 1812 Overture, a piece composed in 1882 to commemorate Napoleon's retreat from Moscow in 1812. It is a very nationalistic piece, involving the French 'La Marseillaise,' Russian folk melodies and, at times, thunderous cannon fire. This first incident happened the year before I came to Eastman, or 1958.

A certain music critic for the local newspaper was assigned the duty of attending all concerts of the Rochester Philharmonic, always occurring on Thursday nights. His custom, however, was to retire to the local pub, quaff a few ales while listening to the live radio broadcast, write his notes for the next day's edition, and depart into the night with no one the wiser. No one, that is, until the following incident became known:

Previous to the concert, little gremlins from the music school gained entry into the Eastman Theatre, where the concert was to take place. Knowing that the 1812 Overture contained simulated cannon blasts, said gremlins crawled up into the structure high above the stage and affixed a fake duck, complete with feathers. That evening, as the conductor led the orchestra to the point in question, the gremlins hid from sight backstage. And when the orchestra reached its first cannon blast - **WHOOOMM!** - the duck came falling out of the rafters, landing with a 'thud' next to Maestro's podium.

The audience was in hysterics, but none of this was known to the music critic from the newspaper. He had no way of knowing the audience was breaking up while the orchestra strained to keep straight faces. (Try doing that while playing a horn). The next day, the critic's published review said nothing of the crashed duck and, with the story now all over town, he was 'reassigned to details other than music' by his superiors. The gremlins' names were whispered in hushed reverence for years and, as far as I know, they were never caught. Good. I hope they do it again sometime.

The second incident involving the 1812 Overture came in 1961, when I was playing horn with the Rochester Philharmonic.

The orchestra played many jobs besides the Thursday night concerts, and this next event was scheduled one evening - IN A FIELD! That's right: the Rochester Philharmonic was playing in a field outside of town, and some local politician (a senator, as I recall) was going to arrive via motorcade during the performance, leap onstage and bless us all with his presence. We couldn't wait, of course, and the 1812 was on the agenda.

When we arrived to set up, risers had been positioned for us to sit on. But as I was finding my place, I noticed something unusual behind and off to one side of us. Howitzers.

Whenever an orchestra is going to perform the 1812 Overture, arrangements have to be made for cannon blasts. Tchaikovsky wrote them into the score. So on stage, in the concert hall, the orchestra will rent little devices that make a lot of noise to simulate this effect. Sometimes they'll even hire actors dressed in period attire to shoot blank musket fire in accompaniment to the simulated cannons. But here, out in this open field, I could see that the orchestra had gone the ultimate: they'd hired the Army who, of course, brought the real thing to the job.

As I unpacked my horn, I kept looking at these things. There were three of howitzers on wheels, each with two chairs behind. And there was one chair out in front of them and - WHAT? WHAT'S THIS? There's a MUSIC STAND in front of the howitzers?

As we neared the beginning of the performance, some Army vehicles arrived. Now, men in battle fatigues marched across the field, their combat boots more suited to the terrain than our polished shoes. One such soldier carried a score under his arm as he called out:

"Hup, two, three, four; hup, two, three, four..."

They came to their post in formation, spun on their heels at the rear of the howitzers, and their commander barked:

"Men - AT EASE!"

Then they sat down ramrod straight in their chairs. The commander situated his score on the music stand, then sat down himself in front of them, likewise ramrod straight. The little music student unpacking his horn didn't know whether to laugh at this or not, so he didn't: howitzers - and a music stand - at a concert? And now the concert was about to begin.

The 1812 was scheduled as the last item on the program, so as we proceeded with the rest of the concert, I kept turning and looking back. This was the first orchestra I'd ever been in that had an artillery section, and I wasn't sure of how to act. I just continued playing the notes as they'd come up in front of me.

Just before the 1812 was about to start, tremendous car horn-blasting could be heard. The senator had arrived, and their motorcade came roaring right up in front of the stage. Grinning ear to ear, this silver-haired dandy leaped onto the stage and said something to the effect of:

"Hello, hello! Although I'm not from your town here, I have fond memories of sitting in the back seat of my daddy's car as he drove through here many years ago!"

(This is an accurate description. I couldn't believe it either when I heard it).

As the senator waxed magniloquent, I turned and looked at the artillery section again. They continued to sit ramrod straight in their chairs, and I was becoming more confused with each passing minute. Finally, the senator was done and the 1812 began.

As the piece started, I noticed the infantrymen remained seated in their chairs. The Army, I concluded, wasn't going to waste energy standing when they didn't have to stand. But then, as we approached the mid-section of the 1812, I noticed they'd assumed active postions behind the howitzers, and the commander was standing behind the music stand - WITH A BATON IN HIS HANDS!

Then, we came to the part in which the cannons are 'played.' Still not able to believe what I could see, I turned in my chair to see what they were going to do next. The commander - wearing ear protectors under his cap and with a straight face - now held the baton in the air, somewhat resembling Toscanini in battle fatigues. And now, at his first cue, he gave a DOWNBEAT TO THE FIRST HOWITZER!

"FA-WHOOOMMM!"

The thing recoiled under the blast, smoke and paper flying out the end as the commander stood to the side, avoiding the concussion, and conducted. And as the men scurried to reload it, he brought in the second cannon with a mighty sweep of the baton:

"FA-WHOOOMMM!"

Now, they were firing in rapid succession, the commander/conductor carving the air with his baton, diving, delving, and swooping as he elicited full performance from his charges:

"FA-WHOOOMMM! FA- WHOOOMMM!..."

The thing that seemed so strange to me was that no one else

seemed to be paying attention to this. Everyone in the orchestra was watching our conductor, who somberly looked out over the scene in progress as if he were somehow invoking Tchaikovsky's spirit...

"FA-WHOOOMMM! FA-WHOOOMMM!...!"

Commander/conductor was in full sway. The cannons were erupting rapid-fire as he railed the men into rapid recharges with his baton:

"Schnell! Accelerando! Ready - PULL...!"

"FA - WHOOOMMM! FA - WHOOOMMM...!"

I eventually watched our conductor bring the piece to a conclusion, and when we all stood during the ensuing applause, I once again turned to view the Army. They were standing next to their cannons at attention, saluting the audience as the smoke drifted off behind them. It seemed strange that their music stand was still there. I thought it should have been blown away during the fusillade.

As we packed our instruments afterwards, I looked up to see them returning to their vehicles in the twilight of the evening:

"Hup, two, three, four; hup, two, three, four..."

The senator was gone, the audience was dispersing, and the little music student stood looking at the remaining howitzers, the empty music stand in front of them, and the still visible smoke drifting off into the night. At the time, I thought something must be wrong with me for thinking this was so weird.

'TILL EULENSPIEGEL'S LUSTIGE STREICHE,'
- and -
THE UNFORTUNATE MAESTRO

The following story went through the Eastman School while I was a student there. Although it happened somewhere else and didn't involve me, the story is too colorful to let slide by unnoticed. For reasons quickly to be obvious, names and locales have been changed.

A certain horn player in a major symphony was known to show up at concerts with a few belts under his own belt. We'll call him Lloyd for now. He could play the horn whether he'd been belting or not, and was widely respected as a musician.

On the day in question, however, Lloyd had apparently had one too many belts, and he arrived onstage slightly dazed from his activities earlier in the day. The orchestra members were not concerned, however. This had happened many times before, and Lloyd always came through. The first number on today's program was 'Till Eulenspiegel's Merry Pranks,' by Richard Strauss.

For the sake of anyone not familiar with the type of music involved in this short anecdote, let me explain briefly what is involved. Richard (pronounced Ree-kard) Strauss was a German romantic composer/conductor, and his orchestral poem 'Till Eulenspiegel's Lustige Streiche' (meaning 'Till Eulenspiegel's Merry Pranks') concerns a happy-go-lucky little character (named Till Eulenspiegel) from German mythology. The piece 'Till Eulenspiegel' opens, after a few gentle bars of violins, with a famous horn solo signaling Till's arrival on the scene. Our man Lloyd was now faced with playing this solo in concert.

Another German romantic composer was Richard Wagner, whose style differed greatly from Strauss'. Wagner used heavy and loud orchestrations to drive home the point in much of his music, compared to the lyric and poetic style achieved by Strauss. I have heard it said that the two are as different as, say, as a folk singer and a rock band. With this in mind, read on.

The world-famous guest conductor now walked onstage to begin the concert. He bowed to the audience's applause, then turned to give the downbeat for 'Till Eulenspiegel.' The violins stroked their opening bars with shimmering delight, then held the chord for Till's horn signal from afar. When the conductor turned to cue in Lloyd, he was slouched down in his chair in a daze.

The conductor was aghast. No other horn player was going to jump in and play the part (orchestra etiquette), and now here they were: the violins were holding the chord and Lloyd was out to lunch! The conductor modestly stopped the performance. (Perhaps no one would notice? Will they think we're just warming up?)

With a mighty rap of the baton, the conductor glared at Lloyd, actually making eye contact with him and conveying his exteme displeasure. Lloyd nodded, signaling that he was ready, so the conductor - none too pleased - began anew.

A second time, the violins stroked their opening bars with shimmering delight and again held the chord, awaiting Till's horn call from afar. And - AGAIN, LLOYD STAYED SLOUCHED DOWN IN HIS CHAIR!

No one else dared to pick up a horn and play the part to cover for Lloyd (it simply isn't done!) and the world-famous guest conductor, by now furious, brought the baton slamming down on the music stand again as he ended the opening for a second time!

This time, however, the conductor was steaming. He pointed to the assistant first horn player and whispered in rage:

"You! You play deese part! You hear? Do you understand me, Herr horn player?"

The assistant first horn (who would have been ME in a different orchestra!) nodded. He understood. The Maestro started the world-famous orchestra now for a third time!

So now, once again, the violins stroked their opening bars with shimmering delight, and now once again (somewhat nervously) they held their chord awaiting Till's anticipated horn call from afar. This time they got results, but not what anyone expected...

...as Maestro gave the cue to the assistant horn player, and as the assistant brought his horn to his lips, some light must have come on in Lloyd's brain. He suddenly realized that the cue was being given, and as the violins continued holding the tremelo, Lloyd whipped up his horn past the astonished assistant and began playing **THE WRONG SOLO!**

This was not the famous horn call from the beginning of 'Till

Eulenspiegel' that the audience patiently awaited. No indeed: Lloyd was belting out the wild horn solo from the beginning of Richard WAGNER'S 'Der Fliegende Hollander,' (The Flying Dutchman)!

True, they were both German/romantic composers, and they were both named 'Richard,' and the horn solos both occurred at the beginning of their respective pieces, but it was the **WRONG SOLO** in the **WRONG PIECE**, and Lloyd sat onstage blasting it out for the entire concert hall to hear!

The only other thing I remember about this incident is that the Maestro went into a rage onstage, shouting, pointing, and ordering that Lloyd be removed from the hall. I only wish I'd been present when this happened, for it seems that the price of admission would have been worth anything to see this whole episode in person.

I was interested, years later, to find Lloyd's name listed in another major symphony. Perhaps he, like Ditmar, resolved his problem with alcohol. Let's hope so, and I certainly hope that I haven't given a clue to who he was or where this happened.

WALTER, I WANT-A YOU TO MEET-A MY FRIEND...

The Sweet Violets Ragtime Band played at the Woodbridge Tavern every Saturday night for about eight years. Its proximity to the Detroit River made it a first stop for rum-runners during the twenties, and now its very rusticness made it a trendy place for all the elite to hang out during a night on the town.

The Journeyman always played solo piano for an hour before being joined by the band for the rest of the night. People would come in, have a sandwich and a beer to ragtime, then sit back and wait for the Sweet Violets to arrive. On the night in question, the place filled up considerably by our nine o'clock starting time.

Walt Gower, the clarinet/soprano sax player, arrived and was unpacking his horns as the Journeyman boogied. There was something else Gower always unpacked also: a chess set. We habitually set the thing up on the piano and played a game of chess as the night progressed. When Gower wasn't playing the clarinet, he was gazing down at the sixty-four squares. When I wasn't too engrossed in thumping out some rhythm, I'd cast a glance at them as well and try to figure out a move. The games, from a purist's point of view, were probably pretty lousy, but the attention it drew was fantastic:

"How can you guys play chess and play music at the same time?" they'd ask.

"We can't," we'd answer, and leave it to them to figure out if that meant anything or not. But now, before we started playing, Gower was complaining about something:

"Hey, Bob. I don't have a barstool to sit on. Every one in the joint is taken."

"Hmm," I mumbled. *"Maybe one will open up."*

"Yeah; let's see," he added, as he continued unpacking horns and bishops.

As the other band members arrived and were setting up, a friend of Gower's came through the door. He brought with him a well-dressed man and a beautiful woman. Gower's friend ran up to him:

"Walter," he said in broken English, and as the Journeyman couldn't help but overhear, *"I have a very-a special honor tonight! I have-a with me - THE ITALIAN CONSUL!"*

We both looked up at the guests, smiled, and waved to the man in the suit, who graciously waved back as he was being escorted to his reserved table. We watched as the consul pulled out the chair for his wife, and now the three of them sat down. Waitresses scurried to accommodate him. He looked pleased with all the attention.

At this point, some obnoxious character showed up at the bandstand. He was upset over the fact that our little stage was in his way. Obviously looking for a fight of some kind, he railed at us over something ridiculously stupid:

"What's this f'ing stage doing here? I'm not going to walk through all those people to get to the bar!"

We finally got rid of him, and now it was time to start playing. But Gower didn't have a barstool yet. Worse, people were sitting on all of them. Finally, a plan:

The band walked over to the bar and nodded politely to the guests who were wondering what we were doing over there. Then, we turned our backs to the bar to face the whole saloon and started playing the Star-Spangled Banner. As everyone patriotically stood up, Gower seized a barstool and we paraded back on-stage. To this day, I don't know if it was the row that erupted afterward or what that caused him to start bringing his own stool, but we never had the problem again.

"Hey Bob! We want to hear 'Indiana' in the worst way!"

The customers always asked - yea, BEGGED - for this number. 'Indiana in the worst way' featured Nate Panicacci, our trumpet player, standing up and blundering his way through the verse. He'd split notes, fracture notes, put the trumpet down on the floor and pretend to stomp it flat, pick it up again and blunder further on into Indiana, even stopping and starting over again when it totally bottomed out. Amazingly, the worse we could play it, the better they liked it. The Italian consul chuckled as he drank his chilled vino, nudging his wife with his elbow. Obviously the diplomat's perfect window-dressing, she just nodded politely and showed little emotion as the men yukked it up.

During our first set, we kept hearing arguments break loose from the jerk who had bothered us earlier. With standing room only, people were lining the walls three or four deep, and this guy was right over there among them, screaming in their faces. They did a pretty good job of ignoring him. But now, some dignitary from the Detroit Symphony had come over to say 'Hi' to us. Walt looked up from the chess game:

"Oh, hi, Charley," he said. "Hey, let me introduce you to the Italian consul. He's sitting over here with a friend of mine. Maybe he'll line up a tour for the symphony."

The band would continue playing as Gower took a parade of people, over the next two hours, to meet the Italian consul. The Journeyman, consul, and everyone else in the place for that matter, suddenly looked up when a wild commotion broke loose along the back wall. The afore-mentioned jerk had opened his mouth one too many times, and now the people standing three deep at the wall seized him en masse, hoisted him over their heads, and hand-over-handed him across the saloon in the direction of the door. A huge cheer went up when he passed just under the transom, arms and legs flailing wildly, and disappeared to the pavement outside.

With the jerk no longer available for a side show, Gower was emphatically bemoaning the fate of his checkmated king. He waved his arms in the air in frustration as people craned their necks to see if they could gain a peek at the final position, but it was for naught. He'd ball up some soggy napkins, bounce them off the floor, and frantically begin resetting up the board as the band thundered on. But now, his friend and the consul were standing there to say 'good night.'

"Good-a night, my friend," said the man with the broken English. "We must-a leave now. Thank-a you for a wonderful time."

Gower bowed politely as now the consul stepped up to thank him also. His lovely wife, of course, did not seem perplexed by the fact that she had to stand aside as the dignitaries moved ahead of her. The consul smiled broadly as he said:

"You are a fine-a musician, Mr. Gower. I hope I can-a come back someday."

Gower bowed again, as the Journeyman and band sat waiting for these people to exit so we could start our next tune. Then, it happened. The beautiful woman stepped up to Gower with one of those expressions on her face that has 'you jerk' written all over it and said in perfect English:

"Thank you for being so kind to my husband, but I am the Italian consul."

With that, she just turned and walked out the door before any one of us could mumble some kind of stupid response. She had, apparently, heard more than enough for one night.

The remainder of the gig was spent with the Journeyman and Gower playing somewhat subdued Dixieland for the fans and even less subdued chess for themselves. When the fans observed us playing our instruments, staring at the chess board, and possibly scratching our heads with a spare hand from time to time, it had nothing to do with concentration on the king's gambit or anything else of the kind. No, indeed. At this point, all we were trying to figure out was how we could be such idiots.

Gower and Milne playing chess
Photo by a sympathetic fan following
the departure of the Italian consul

'SEE YOU ON THE PIANO BENCH'

I very rarely ever give piano lessons to anyone, and the following story is one of the reasons why.

Lynn Evans and her husband Ken moved from Seattle to this area in the late 1970's. The two of them are enormously in love and it's obvious. His job was with General Motors and she had not yet become the director of sales for the Ramada Inn, a post she held for years.

One night, when I was playing at Charley's Crab, Lynn came in and asked me to teach her how to play a tune. She had bought a piano (which she didn't know how to play) and wanted to surprise her husband by playing and singing I HONESTLY LOVE YOU for his birthday. The only time she could have lessons and keep this a surprise, of course, was when he was at work. In a moment of blunderous non-thinking, I agreed to this foolhardy idea.

Her piano was located right next to the front door of the condo, and after about the third lesson she was doing fairly well. One day, as we both sat on the piano bench following the notes on the page, we heard the sound of the door opening in the hallway. Lynn screamed:

"Oh my God! Kenny had a doctor appointment this afternoon, and he's come home instead of going back to work! I've got to hide you!"

She grabbed me from the bench, shoving me into the closet behind the front door. My first thought was, "Is this a 'B' rated movie?"

I heard Ken come in and say 'hello' to her, and then I heard her saying "Oh, let me take your coat for you, honey." But then he said:

"No, dear, I'll hang it up myself."

Inside the closet, I knew what was going to happen, and it did. He opened the friggin' door to hang up his coat and what to his wondering eyes did appear but the most idiotic feeling piano player in North America, cringing, looking stupid, and trying to think of something appropriate to say.

"Uh, hi Ken," I mumbled somewhat weakly.

Ken busted up laughing. He immediately realized what Lynn was up to and he invited me to stay longer. The Journeyman Piano Player, however, couldn't get out the door fast enough.

Ever since this embarrassing incident, over ten years ago, Lynn has never said 'goodbye' to me. She always laughs and says *'I'll see you on the piano bench!'*

...And I still cringe, every time she says it.

A FAMILY AFFAIR?

During the mid 70's, Bob Seeley and myself were the piano players at the Clamdigger's Restaurant in Farmington Hills. We alternated; one of us would play a cocktail hour, the other would play later into the evening.

Among our patrons were many people who worked at a local T.V. station in Southfield, including T.V. host Vic Caputo. Vic was doing a series of local interviews for the station, and he decided to interview Seeley and myself for his show. Consequently, I walked in one day to find T.V. cameras and huge lights set up all around the piano. Caputo and cohorts were having a good time sitting around the piano bar, and when I began playing I expected them to start with their interview right away. They didn't. In fact, the cameras and T.V. paraphernalia quietly became part of the general scenery as people came in, had a drink at the piano, and then were seated for dinner. Two hours went by before Vic decided to start the interview.

Caputo, with microphone, moved to the end of the piano bar to my right, a pair of picturesque diners in a booth behind him having been selected for backdrop. The stunning lady and man had just been served their stuffed lobsters when the cameras and lights came on.

"Good evening, everyone," said Caputo, smiling as he faced into the three cameras and glaring lights. *"This is Vic Caputo on location at - THE CLAMDIGGER'S RESTAURANT!"*

Everyone broke into a wild cheer for the introduction. Everyone, that is, but the stunning lady and gentleman sitting behind him. They looked up in mid-bite when the lights came on, their eyes wide with horror. When they saw the cameras broadcasting the two of them back into their respective living rooms, the man went diving out of the booth onto the floor to get out of sight. The lady didn't hit the floor, but spun out of that booth and was gone faster than anything I'd ever seen before. Two steaming stuffed lobster dinners, partially eaten, and wine left quivering in the stemware were all that remained of the backdrop.

Caputo was masterful. He never even flinched as they tripped over cables running for the door:

"Tonight we are proud to bring into your living rooms two area pianists..."

He didn't take his eyes off the camera when they hit the massive double doors, fleeing in haste:

"...who play for the dining and entertainment pleasure of most, if not all, our distinguished guests..."

The diners never even looked back as they fled to somewhere more private to continue whatever it was they were discussing. And as they hoped, I'm sure, that no one at home had the T.V sets on, hmmmMM?

I've often wondered if they ever came back. I think Vic wanted to interview them next. Godspeed; godspeed.

THE GREAT NORTHERN FISHING SHANTY EXPEDITION

I learn a lot about people while playing pianos in public. People come in and talk to me, generally relating interesting stories told in interesting ways. The Journeyman Piano Player learns to play piano (to keep his boss happy) while he listens and talks (to keep customers happy) at the same time. This following story is one that unfolded over several nights sometime around 1978. Although I've heard plenty of stories more bizarre than this, this particular one has remained with me for a lot of years, for some reason. Maybe it belongs to Lake Wobegon, I don't know. Oh well; here goes:

People tend to take certain things for granted, never suspecting that what is plain and mundane to one person is unique and legendary to someone else.

Take, for instance, ice fishing shanties. Fishing shanties are no more than a pile of otherwise unusable plywood and boards, hammered and pounded into some kind of configuration that will stand up in the wind and hopefully float when the ice melts. Their only requirement, as far as I know, is that the owner's name be painted on the sides in letters so huge that township officials can read them from boats when the thing lies on the bottom. That way, they know who to send the removal bill to.

One January, when I was playing at Charlie's Crab, a car salesmen convention from California was being held nearby. Every night at the piano I was hearing stories from them about how they were enjoying Michigan, for most of them had never been here. Then one night they told me about the tour they had lined up for the next day; the tour bus was taking them to Lake Orion and other nearby inland lakes on a guided tour of fishing shanties, the curious custom they'd heard about ever since childhood in California.

"*Fishing shanties?*" I queried, not sure that I understood correctly. At first I thought they were going ice fishing, but no; they wanted a guided tour of fishing shanties, the same as most people ride the tour bus through Washington D.C. ("And on your right, ladies and gentlemen, the Capitol of the United States of America!")

I couldn't believe it, so I asked one of them ('Doug' was his name) just why the hell would anyone come thousands of miles to go to Lake Orion and look at ramshackled piles of boards dragged out onto the ice, and sporting such ingenious witticisms on their sides as 'Beam Me Up, Scotty; This Place Sucks.' Doug, however, told me in all seriousness that he'd heard stories of fishing shanties in California ever since he was a kid, he had also seen pictures of them in magazines, and somehow all of this intrigued him in such a way that he was actually excited now about the prospect of seeing one the next day. It was like a dream fulfilled, or something like that.

"FISHING SHANTIES?"

I relayed to him the true story that happened to some guys I knew in high school who had put a pot-bellied stove inside a fishing shanty. When it went through the ice, the explosion literally blasted the shanty full of ice-water, sending the afore-mentioned bimbos crashing from their orange crates. Other than resembling ice men of the Himalayas by the time they reached their cars, the idiots actually survived unscathed.

This story only heightened Doug's excitement. Suddenly he was aware of the potential dangers in north-country shantying, and I know he retold my story with embellishments on the tour bus.

So now, gentle readers, try to imagine for yourselves what the Journeyman Piano Player was imagining the the next day:

...A bus pulls up to a frozen lake where thirty or forty Porta-John look-a-likes sit around on the ice, and the tour guide now intones solemnly over whirring video cameras:

"...And on your right, ladies and gentlemen, is one of the strange, unexplainable customs peculiar to the northern states. These grizzled woodsmen risk their lives, day in and day out, in a pursuit so arcane as to be beyond the understanding of civilized Californians..."

If only they knew that inside most of these shacks, the grizzled woodsmen sat drinking beer and playing cards, while the fishing poles stood stacked in the corner.

PLAY ONE FER' ME, KID

"So ya' think ya' wanna play the piano fer a livin', kid? Well, sid-down and listen up already. Maybe we can change yer sputterin' mind a-fore it's too friggin' late!"

Sometimes I wish someone had said that to me before this all started. It seems that the piano business is romanticized in movies, a la Humphrey Bogart and Sam in Casablanca, while the reality of it is better described by unprintable graffiti sprayed on bridge underpasses. Consider the following scenario, true facts taken from a finer dining establishment in a ghetto area where the Journeyman Piano Player and the band were forced by economics to shovel up some gas money. For openers, consider that we would only play during daylight hours. Band and customers were gone way ahead of dusk.

SCENE ONE: A mid-summer's day. You're at a corner bar in a seedy area, downtown Detroit. Outside, filthy children play in the street while winos weave their way from sidewalk to street to sidewalk. A greasy, oil-drenched man working under his car across the street crawls out and goes into his house in search of a particular tool. The sun beats down.

INSIDE: While playing blues, the Journeyman Piano Player (J.P.P) and his quick-draw associate on the banjo (Q.D.A.) sat chording along and lazily looking out the door while other members of the band wailed the strains. In the summer heat, we watched with no real concern as two cars pulled up in front of a house a short distance away.

As the trumpet rose to the melodic note-bending of a true southern blues, policemen in riot gear suddenly burst from the cars and raced to the porch of a house. With one smash of the battering ram, the door was gone and the cops were inside. The trumpet wailed on as J.P.P. and Q.D.A. looked at each other with raised eyebrows, and while the customers, not able to see the proceedings outside, hung on every note from the band.

COMMENT HEARD INSIDE: *"Isn't there any *!#@%*@ service in this place?"*

As patrons enthusiastically cheered the trumpet winding down its solo, the clarinet's haunting sound took over as J.P.P. and Q.DA. watched with dishpan-sized eyes. The police were now running around the outside of the house, shotguns in hand, bulletproof vests in place and magnum pistols at their sides. Boys will be boys.

COMMENT YELLED ACROSS THE ROOM: *"If ya' want a beer, get up off yer arsan' get one!"*

The crowd was almost on its feet as the clarinet trailed off and the tailgate trombone unleashed a few train-horn-sounding opening notes to its solo. The other instruments all backed up the tingling slow melody crawling forth from the slide-bone. J.P.P. and Q.D.A. watched in disbelief as the wards of the house across the street now became wards of the Big House across the town, slowly parading down the stairs at gunpoint with their cuffed hands behind them. More cops in riot-gear politely opened doors to their waiting vehicles.

COMMENT: *"Go *#!* yourself with your beer! I brought my own!"*

RETURN COMMENT: *"I hope you gag on it!"*

The Journeyman Piano Player declined to play a solo when his turn came, and now the band wound up the final chorus with a mighty, growling blues ensemble that surely moved the heart and soul of everyone in the place. Everyone, that is, except J.P.P. and Q.D.A., for they were still staring ga-ga-eyed out the door as the cops drove their hood-laden cars around the corner right past our noses and disappeared down the street. The summer sun continued to drench the area in rays. Had a mirage taken place?

The tune had ended and as the crowd roared its approval, a man with a paper bag came down the street looking for bottles, the children still played at curbside, a woman walked by with a bag of groceries, and the guy across the street came back with the right tool for his car. He crawled underneath again to continue putting the thing back together.

And the customers applauded on and on.

"So come over here, kid. Get a taste of some of this fer' yerself. Sid-down right here on the ol' piano stool. That's it; just turn the ol' seat to bring it up a little higher. Ya' wanna' play a few? Go ahead, heh-heh. Yeah, go ahead. Play a slow one fer' me, kid. Play a slow one. Hey, that sounds good. You got it, kid; you got it... "

THE CHICAGO PIANO

The professional pianist is constantly being told by owners and managers what to play and how to play it. They seem to think that the musician is an extension of their own musically bankrupt brain, and that their ideas should take precedence over the years, talent, and training of the poor devil pushing down the notes. This once prompted the me to obtain barf bags from the airport and place them among the condiments of a finer-dining establishment in which I was playing. I had written the following on the bags:

R. MILNE for your listening enjoyment

These bags for your convenience

But it doesn't end there, of course. The serious student of piano studies the various ways piano jobs end as well as begin. This is similar to the way archaeologists study the end of the dinosaur era, noting that pianos in restaurants are becoming about as rare as dinosaurs walking around in the woods. Consider the following likeness to the 'Big Bang' theory:

You're in Chicago, early 1960's. You've entered a hoity-toity joint that features finer dining. Now you've walked up the grand staircase to the second level and have been seated at a table featuring sterling silver and stem-ware. A tuxedo-clad waiter, who introduces himself as your 'captain,' immediately arrives and demands your order, his staff of lackeys filling your water glasses as he elicits your responses without adieu. You are intimidated by his authoritative manner, but now you relax a bit as you notice the approach of the piano player.

'The approach of the piano player?' you ask. *'Yes'*, I answer, for Jerome (not his real name - he didn't want this story publicized) is now approaching you on a motorized piano cart that circulates among the tables. He smiles and tinkles on the useless spinet, enhancing the

evening with fairy-fingered renditions of hackneyed tunes which the management has deemed appropriate for their diners. (*"Don't push down too many notes at once, Jerome. It's distracting!"*) Jerome wears a plastered-on smile to disguise his gin-plastered brain as he plays at the rate of fourteen notes per minute, then puts the cart in reverse and departs. Your 'captain' strides up with salads and commands you to enjoy them.

The tomato wedge is excellent, and your date is noticing that the lettuce hearts are just perfect. You gaze into her eyes; she gazes into yours. And then -

A horrendous crash erupts. Diners are sitting upright in their chairs as they look around in amazement. Suddenly, people are jumping up and running. Jerome, in his don't-give-a-damn drunken condition, has backed the piano cart over the edge of the grand staircase, sending him flying backwards down the stairs while the useless spinet did cartwheels after him. Of course, when he hit the bottom, the thing came crashing over his legs, breaking one.

'And now - YOUR STEAKS!'

Your captain is grinning ear to ear as he arrives with entourage for the table-side flambe' of your dinners. Packs of lackeys are setting up plate-warmers as he presents the raw filets to you. Before placing them on the flames, he informs with imposing authority:

'These are the finest pieces of meat that money can buy!'

He seems annoyed that you are looking in the other direction to see what has happened to the piano player. He frowns as you watch them placing Jerome on a stretcher. He ignores them as they trundle the useless spinet off to the side. When you look back at the steaks, he taps them with a cooking fork and smiles. He is pleased that he has your complete attention, but now he is frowning again. The sirens outside are disturbing him.

THE NIGHT OF THE GREEN GODDESS

As may be imagined, some of the scenes that erupt unexpectedly in the pursuit of gracious dining are ribald. It has been my observation, after thirty years of playing in everything from dirt-floor whiskey-swilling barrel houses to gold-chandeliered mansions, that you can't buy class. People, whether they're millionaires in silk or shop-rats in denims, have behavior patterns that they adhere to. Some rise to the occasion, while others sink to it. Consider the following scenario:

It was at the Sundog Restaurant in Dearborn, 1974. The clientele was high-class. Even the president of Ford Motor Co. dropped by now and then. Women displayed their latest styles and fashions as they hung around in the evening, and the Journeyman Piano Player played in the bar area for both seated diners and others who were awaiting their table reservations.

Various celebrities were regular clients. Mike was one celebrity in particular. He was a standout with the Detroit Lions football team, and his well-developed Adonis figure was noticed by many of the fashionable women as well. Mike liked this. He often invited them to sit with him for drinks, dinner, and more. They loved it.

On the night of the Green Goddess salad dressing, the bar area was filled with diners. Mike was seated at the bar with several friends. They'd been drinking and having fun. Suddenly, a gorgeous blonde woman came into the bar from one of the other dining rooms. She was, uh, to put it politely, well out in front of herself when she came through the door.

Mike looked up, smiled and waved. She recognized him immediately, for it turned out they were old friends, and now Mike's buddies were making room for her to sit next to him at the bar. With flourish, another round of drinks was ordered. The Journeyman Piano Player played on. Nothing was unusual, yet.

About fifteen minutes later, some guy came wandering in from the dining room looking for his date. There was a scene when he found her hanging on Mike, nose in his ear. After a brief interlude of screaming and yelling, the man stormed out of the place. The diners, bartenders, and Journeyman Piano Player tried to pretend they hadn't noticed.

Serious drinking took place over the next hour, as did serious body-fondling. Mike and the blonde had rediscovered each other's tongues, and they had both consumed enough alcohol that they were sure no one would notice where their hands were on each other. The diners pace of eating had slowed as the two at the bar, their backs to the rest of the place, were sure no one would notice him caressing her mountainous front while his cohorts roared with laughter. The bartenders stood polishing glasses, trying to look the other way. Journeyman Piano Player was having trouble thinking of appropriate tunes to play. He'd already played 'All of Me.'

Waitresses were trying to act nonchalant as they scurried from table to table. Journeyman Piano Player noticed how one in particular was able, incredibly, to keep her eyes on the people she was talking to when Mike pushed the blonde's sweater up to rest on top of her, uh, massive femininities. The waitress' expression never flinched as she spoke with the people, while Mike now had both the femininities in full grip at the bar. The cohorts were in hysterics and the bartenders could no longer conceal their laughter. The blonde loved it and the Journeyman Piano Player was beating the hell out of the keys as he tried to create some kind of distraction.

If recollection serves correctly, possibly fifteen minutes passed as diners became conditioned to the level of adoration now taking place. People were actually still eating dinner, albeit nervously, and only casting occasional glances at the two good friends renewing their acquaintance. It was then that a waitress came from the kitchen carrying salads to her table.

As she breezed down the bar with the large tray at shoulder height, Mike, bleary-eyed as he was, turned to see what was going by. He saw the salads and little dishes of salad dressings on the tray, right under his nose. Unbeknownst to the waitress, but in full sight of the diners and piano player, he lifted a dish with Green Goddess salad dressing from her tray.

The events of the next few seconds were mind-boggling. Mike immediately lifted his friend's bra to display the full nature of nuturing and annointed her ends with Green Goddess. Then, as forks fell from hands and chords crashed into dissonances, Mike seized her by the shoulders and proceeded eating the Green Goddess from where it hung. The blonde was in ecstasy, for the booze had obviously made both of them unaware of where they were or what was happening, and the cohorts lay on their faces on the bar, tears of laughter coming from their eyes as they pounded the bar again and again with their fists.

Unfortunately, there is no more that I can tell to this story, for the Journeyman Piano Player was almost trampled by the mob as we all ran for the doors before someone called the police. Customers actually chased me through the kitchen, that being the closest point of exit, and on out into the alley to find their ways back to the valet.

The only other thing I can add happened the following night. I returned to the Sundog still in a state of shock, and had been playing for about half an hour when I looked up to see Mike coming through the door. He was immaculate in his three-piece Italian-cut suit, and his entrance was as nonchalant as anyone could imagine. He strolled through the diners at their tables on his way to the bar and paused in front of the piano. Journeyman Piano Player played 'O Sole Mio' for him, no pun intended. Mike stopped and nodded pleasantly as he said with a straight face:

"*Good evening, Bob. How are you tonight?*"
"*I'm fine,*" I answered, without embellishment. "*And you, sir?*"
"*Excellent,*" he replied.

With that, he walked casually to the bar, found a seat, and raised his hand to signal the bartender, sitting down as if nothing had happened. Absolutely nothing at all.

THE CLUB ROCHESTER

I was playing piano at the Club Rochester one night around 1968 while the owner, Ben Hazleton, (an Archie Bunker look-alike) sat at a table right in front of me smoking a cigar and reminiscing with one of his cronies.

The Club was a long, narrow place that ran from the street entrance all the way to the back alley, and specialized in choice steaks. The long bar started near the back door and ran halfway to the street, creating a train-like dining-car effect. The piano was situated near the rear entrance door, from where the Journeyman Piano Player tried to enhance the candle-lit tables, hanging globe lamps, and savory smells with a few chords and tunes.

Ben leisurely oversaw his restaurant as he and his friend puffed on, only chuckling slightly to himself when the barmaid slapped some character's face and told him to watch his mouth. Ben liked a little pizazz in the place. It was good for business, too.

As the diners dined and the smokers smoked, the back door could be heard to be bumbling open in some awkward manner. Mumbled curses combined with mechanical noises worked their way inside as the patrons now turned to see what was happening. Suddenly, and with a humongous *'RooOOAAR,'* a motorcycle blasted out of the back entranceway and appeared next to the piano, one of the local yahoos firmly astride it. Now, and with a mighty *'Yee-haaa!'*, he gunned the engine and went flying down the bar past the elegant steak-diners, wheeling among tables and leaving a trail of blue smoke hanging in rings around the globe lights. With customer screams, curses, and much exhaust-gagging temporarily replacing the piano notes, the night-rider went roaring through the place toward the front exit:

"Ye-haa!" "Rumm-rumm."

The Journeyman Piano Player had frozen in mid-chord, not knowing what to think. Ben had only taken one quick look over his shoulder, then returned to his cigar without comment as diners leaped from their chairs in amazement.

"Ye-haa!" could be heard in the distance as he disappeared out the front door.

Noting that Ben and his friend hadn't even reacted to this and were nonchalantly smoking stogies, I could do nothing but continue playing the piano. I strummed a few chords as the scene returned to normality, and it was about two minutes later that Ben's friend finally said something:

"Hey Ben, I think someone just rode a motorcycle through your place."

The unflappable Hazleton took a long drag on his cigar, exhaled slowly, and whimsically replied:

"Yeah... I think it was a Yamaha."

Working at Club Rochester was truly a bizarre experience. Ben was extremely successful with the place, and he was also his own best customer. He loved to sit and drink with his friends, tell stories, listen to more stories, and just have a good time in general. As I would play the piano, he would get out on the dance floor with all the ladies and have a good-natured 'trip the lights fantastic' turn among the other dancing patrons.

One time in particular, he had danced with every lady in sight and now, as a self-intended joke, he was dancing with the broom. I would look up from time to time and see him go waltzing by, eyes shut in bliss, twirling and pirouetting as I played perhaps either the Blue Danube or the Tennessee Waltz. Ben was the archetypical ballroom glider.

As I played, and as he waltzed, a woman that was known to all of us came up to the piano with a request that she wanted to sing. When she started singing, however, she didn't turn to the audience and sing, but rather leaned over the spinet piano to sing into my face. I played on, and she leaned further and further into my face as I tried to lean further and further away from her.

But now, Ben was squinting in my direction as he waltzed. He could see that I having to endure something out of the ordinary with this woman, but he also saw it from a totally different perspective than I did. I was looking into her face as she sang, but all Ben could see was her rear end bent over the piano towards his dining and dancing guests. Alas, I unfortunately knew what he was going to do, and so did everyone else seated at tableside eating steaks for they stopped munching as he drew near her. Ben was going to meet the 'out of ordinary' with something equally 'out of ordinary.'

I now watched him dancing closer and closer as this woman continued to sing into my face, and when I saw him lower the broom handle and point it where the sun never shines, I drew back even further. And now, when her eyes popped wide open and her jaw fell almost to her chest, the scream that I had to withstand was ear-splitting. Ben had shoved the broom handle into her butt and now stood cackling in glee behind her, moving the thing to and fro, to and fro, lifting her high-heel spikes off the floor in the process.

When the screaming subsided, the Journeyman Piano Player was hiding at the bar with his old friend Harry Schemer. Ben was beside himself, tears of laughter pouring from his eyes, and the woman had somehow - amazingly - found humor in the whole thing. She laughed with everyone else and returned to her table as the juke box now came on and gracious dining once again resumed in the Club Rochester.

Harry liked to play the tuba. In fact, it was a Sousaphone that he played in the National Guard Band, but occasionally we'd see him show up at the hostess stand dressed in a three-piece suit and nonchalantly wearing the tuba. When the hostess would approach with a puzzled look on her face, he'd casually mention:

"Table for one, my dear. I am dining alone tonight."

Harry was able to keep a straight face as she'd escort him to his table where he'd sit down, put on his glasses, pick up the menu, study it, and all the while wearing the tuba. When the waiter would set down a water glass, Harry would signal that he wanted two. After the waiter obliged, Harry would take a sip as he casually studied the menu, and then reach up and throw the second glass of water down the tuba. Replacing the glass on the table with a straight face, he'd now signal that he was ready to order.

"It'll be steak tonight, young man," he'd say, *"and I'll have a gin and tonic if you don't mind. And bring another one for Marmalade, also if you don't mind."*

The confused waiter would place the steak order and return with two drinks. Harry would casually sip one while reading the stock pages of the Wall Street Journal now, and also as the whole place kept their eyes on the second gin and tonic. The waiter would show up with the steak finally, and Harry would politely thank him. Then:

"Well, here goes, Marmalade," and he'd toss the second gin and tonic down the tuba. Replacing the glass on the table, he'd then proceed to leisurely dine in elegance as everyone in the place wondered just what the hell was going on in here.

I would periodically look up at this sight with a puzzled expression, and when Harry had finished eating (and was gently tidying himself with the napkin) I'd look his way and say, somewhat sheepishly:

"*Excuse me, sir.*"

Harry would pretend not to hear, and the other diners would see me trying to get his attention.

"*Excuse me, sir - SIR?*" I'd repeat.

Now Harry would look in my direction, and say:

"*Are you talking to me, young man?*"

"*Uh, yes, sir,*" I'd reply.

"*Well, what is it you want?*" he inquired, imperiously.

"*Well, uh, sir,*" I'd continue, "*I was just wondering, uh... DO YOU PLAY THE TUBA?*"

As Harry sat there looking stunned, the place would usually realize by now that we were pulling a gag, and Harry would be replying to me, somewhat annoyed:

"*The tuba? Why do you ask?*"

"*Well, I, uh, duh...*" I'd mumble, but he'd cut me off:

"*Oh, for Pete's sake! If you HAVE to know, then YES, I HAVE played the tuba! But isn't this rather rude?*"

He'd then arise from his table, come over to the piano and signal the waiter:

"*Sir! Yes, you over there! I'll have another drink, if you don't mind. And bring another one for Marmalade, also if you don't mind!*"

We'd then start playing everything from Jada to the Stars and Stripes Forever. Customers would be sending drinks to the band, but there was always an extra drink for Marmalade, which Harry fired down the tuba at an increasing rate of speed proportional to the lateness of the hour. Beer, whiskey, vodka, soda tonics and mixers of all kinds were dumped down it in the course of any given evening, and every now and then he'd take it five steps to the back alley to empty the thing out, then return to thunder on.

On certain occasions, Harry would have to return in the morning to rescue Marmalade from the beer cases in the back room, where she had been unceremoniously heaved during the previous nights debauchery, temporarily forgotten as her mentors went roaring off after-hours to some egg diner down by Paint Creek.

These nights were always spectacular, but sometimes our fun got cut short. Ben Hazleton would be having so much fun with the customers as they swapped stories about various bars, that he'd periodically fill a bag with whiskey, assign someone to carry a case of beer, and then parade everyone out the back door and into his motor home. Now Ben, and all our paying customers, would go roaring off into the night to some place or other they'd been talking about, leaving myself, Harry, the bartenders and the waiters as the only ones left in the joint while the owner partied on. We'd usually sit and play cards until closing time.

One evening I came in to play at the Club and discovered that a strange event had taken place only hours before I arrived. It seems that during the afternoon lull, a few people were sitting around eating when the front door opened up and six characters came in carrying a coffin. To everyone's horror, it was relayed that a popular waitress in town had died and requested a wake to be held at the Club Rochester. They placed the coffin on the bar, opened it for viewing, and then started drinking at a table next to her. The dining customers didn't know what to think, with pieces of steak firmly stuck on forks but no one wanting to eat them. The prevailing mood took an immediate nosedive.

But then, someone noticed something strange. As the six men sat drinking, boo-hooing, drinking, condoling, drinking, wailing, and drinking, someone noticed a smile on the waitress' face. Closer scrutiny revealed that she was giggling under her breath. Even closer scrutiny revealed that this whole thing was a hoax, the waitress was very much alive, and the Club Rochester had been HAD by another crazy prank dreamed up by equally crazy people.

The six characters had to quickly arise and depart with the coffin before the dining customers could come to their feet, slamming the lid shut and running like hell for the door. I arrived shortly afterward to learn that another adventure in gracious dining had taken place at the Club Rochester.

But this was not the last of the insane, wild-west type capers that went on in this place. Now it was the Rochester sesquicentennial. Everyone was wearing beards, riding horses through town, and drinking. Don't forget the latter - drinking.

The Club was unusually busy during the afternoon, and an apron-clad Hazleton was behind the bar doing diddly as he shot the breeze with his friends while the barmaids ran their butts off trying to keep up. The festivities had everyone in a gala mood as locals partied and carried on, starting roughly at the end of lunch hour and continuing on as long as they could remain standing. Morning business hours were simply a formality that had to be endured until lunch. May God have mercy on unwitting out-of-towners.

I happened to be in Hazleton's one afternoon fooling around with the piano when a familiar sound from this farm-town community made itself known; horses whinnying. Unperturbed, I continued plunking the keys until suddenly there was more and louder whinnying, and now we all looked up to see yahoos riding in through the back door, ducking as they came under the entranceway. John Wayne couldn't have entered more grandiosely, and Ben simply stood puffing cigar and polishing a glass, observing their arrival without expression.

The obviously smashed guests alighted from their steeds and tied them to the bar rail, where one now pounded both fists on the bar as he yelled:

"Ben, we want some GIN!"

Hazleton didn't even smile as he nodded approval, turned, and began pouring the drinks. In the meantime, lunch-time guests wearing business suits and fine dresses were madly pulling their tables and dinners away from the ever shifting position of the horses' rear ends. The punishment for not doing so would be both obvious and merciless, for horses passing water and fire hoses have something very much in common. Of course, even worse threats came to mind as the high-strung animals shifted back and forth:

"Great God! What if the things were to take a..."

Ben turned around and set the drinks down on the bar. Without as much as giving recognition to the the nervous steeds, he added:

"This is a good day. I think I'll have one with you," whereupon he turned back around and poured himself one. The mayhem of people running with tables continued.

Hazleton now turned to the men, drink in hand. They toasted each other and drank, plunking the empties down with a resonating 'thud' on the bar.

Ben nonchalantly looked around the bar, filled with people running wildly carrying dinners, chairs and tables. Then he proved just how equal he was to the occasion. He looked his guests straight in the eye as they wiped their mouths and said:

"Well, gentlemen, what's new?"

By way of serendipity, I will lead you into the eventual demise of the Club Rochester, but first let me explain to the uninitiated just how it is that piano jobs come to sometimes grotesque ends.

When the boss says, 'Will you step into my office, please', do you get the sudden anxious notion that maybe it's all over? That you have been replaced? Today is your last day? Well, dear people, if this has ever happened to you, then you've had more notice than most piano players get when the end is nigh. Consider the following examples:

SCENE 1: It was the late 1960's. One particular joint in Pontiac had hired myself and Bob Seeley to play what was left of their upright piano. We took turns playing alternate nights.

I recall one night in which the customers were so enthused that they passed a derby hat among themselves to generously tip the piano player. (Embarrassing, but it happens sometimes). Beaucoup money could be seen protruding from within as a lady circulated it among the patrons. When the hat reached me, however, all the cash had disappeared except for seven dollars lying in the bottom.

Two nights later, old lizard-fingers Seeley arrived at the appointed hour to begin playing, only to find that the state had padlocked the joint. Signs proclaiming such bons mots as 'SEIZED FOR TAX FORFEITURE,' and 'THIS PROPERTY OWNED BY THE STATE OF MICHIGAN,' covered the door. Seeley was furious, and I had to explain to him in his rage why it would be useless to attempt to get paid for the night from these people. If the state couldn't get paid, the piano player is surely screwed.

Years later I bumped into the cook from this place. He told me how the owner, apparently disgruntled over seeing a hat full of cash going to the piano player, stole the money from the derby as well as money from other sources, and had disappeared from town. End of job, end of joint.

SCENE 2: Sy Richards, great pianist from Cleveland, is well-known by anyone who ever attended the Toronto Ragtime Bashes in the 70's and 80's. He is a quiet, distinguished gentlemen who sports a Tolstoy-type beard and wavy, brushed-back black hair. Extremely aware of his appearance, he takes great care in the selection of his fine, subdued, three-piece suits.

After picking up a job playing at the Cleveland Airport lounge on Sunday afternoons, Sy arrived one particular Sunday to perform. With quiet elegance he moved to the grand piano in the middle of the room. Artists such as Sy do not force their presence upon people, but rather try to blend into the situation at hand and 'hide,' if you will, amidst their music. Sy nodded self-consciously to the table next to him as he sat down. He raised the cover from the keys and studied them as he listened in his head for the opening notes and chords with which to make his entrance. It was then that he noticed 'IT.'

'IT' was the managers. They were standing at Sy's right, grinning from ear to ear while holding up the rabbit suit for him to wear. That's right. A rabbit suit, complete with whiskers, long ears, and a cotton tail. It was Easter, and the idiots had decided they wanted a rabbit to be playing the piano.

The gentle Sy tried to explain why he couldn't wear it.

"NONSENSE!" they said. *"JUST TRY IT ON! IT'LL LOOK GREAT ON YOU!"*

(Note they said *'IT'LL look great on YOU'*, not *'YOU'LL look great in IT.'*)

"B - b - but I'm not a rabbit," he tried to reason. *"I can't wear that thing!"*

Grinning and yukking it up, they tried to fit it on him right there at the piano:

"Just take off that jacket, Mr. Richards. This'll slide right over your clothes."

Sy recalls them standing in the middle of the room still holding the stupid thing in their hands as he went out the door, never to return.

SCENE 3: It was early Thursday evening, about 6:00. The Journeyman Piano Player was driving south into town to play at the Club Rochester. The summer sky was a beautiful blue. Ten miles north of town, J.P.P. noticed something in the air. *"Hmm,"* he thought. *"Farmers must be burning off a field."*

Drawing closer to town, J.P.P noticed that the farm fields were now behind him while the column of smoke was still before him. *"Hmm,"* he thought. *"Fire department must be having a practice drill somewhere."*

Driving now into the downtown section, J.P.P. noticed that Main Street was cordoned off by heavy trucks and equipment. Smoke, resembling Mt. St. Helens at its final eruption, rose from the center of town. *"Hmm,"* he thought. *"The chicken bar-b-que isn't until next week. I'd best check this out."*

J.P.P parked his car and ran several blocks through churning mobs and fleeing people. Upon arriving across the street from the Club Rochester, he saw that it was flaming to the skies under useless water-arches coming from the fire department. Ben Hazleton had come running out the front door past the men with axes, fire hoses, water-gear and fire hats and was now standing at the curb yelling, to the everlasting amazement of all who witnessed it:

"LAST CALL! LAST CALL FOR ALCOHOL AT THE CLUB ROCHESTER!"

After several minutes, the Journeyman Piano Player returned to his car, drove fifty miles further to Detroit, and commenced looking for another job as his previous one burned to the ground.

And no. Of course I didn't have bar-b-cue for dinner that night.

Last call for alcohol at the Club Rochester
Photo by Van Skiver, Pontiac Press, 1970
Courtesy of Rochester Hills Library

PIANOS BY THE POUND

The owner of the tourist trap near Chesapeake Bay stood five-foot-five and weighed some 300 pounds.

The upright piano had been acquired, if that's the right word, the previous year and was situated in the upstairs section of this joint. I should probably say 'discarded the previous year' because I thought our country had anti-dumping laws, but I won't go into that here.

The piano suffered from many deficiencies. For instance, the hammers hit only two of the three strings at once, thus diminishing its volume by thirty-three percent. Various keys either hung up or didn't work, and the basketball-shaped owner simply told me with a wave of his hand:

"Use other notes, kid. You've got plenty of other notes there."

Where was Air Jordan to slam-dunk this imbecile?

The same fat owner had publicized his out-of-town ragtime pianist to a great extent. He even arranged a televised interview that included feeding the interviewer all kinds of wrong information about me, which I now had to field on live television network:

"I hear you've played all over the country, Mr. Milne."

"No sir, I have not."

After the on-camera episode was cut short, local people from the bay area came in droves to hear the pianist at Fat Albert's (not the real name, of course). Having only seen a few brief seconds of the televised interview, they had erroneously assumed they tuned in on the tail end of it. And now, as they poured in through the doors, I was supposed to keep the keys from hanging up and produce something worth listening to from this antiquated junk pile. Patrons ooh-ed and ahh-ed to each contorted attempt, thinking it was part of the act. I mumbled something under my breath to the owner as he waddled by concerning the condition of the piano:

"Yeah, yeah, I'll get it fixed," was all he'd say.

As the weeks wore on, it was obvious that he was getting tired of hearing my comments, polite as I tried to submit them. It became increasingly obvious that he was 'very busy, very busy,' and that I was simply annoying him with my attempts to make the piano something that people might want to listen to.

Finally, with aching arms and fingers, I was forced to tell him again that the piano needed serious help. After avoiding and running away from me for some fifteen minutes in the middle of his restaurant,

I finally caught him at table-side long enough to explain my plight. Now, due to the fact that he couldn't ignore me in front of customers, he listened for a moment. Then he thought for a moment. Then he put his fat hands on his hips and stood glaring at me for yet another moment. Finally, he erupted, screaming and yelling to the astonishment of his lunch-time guests:

"What do you mean it's not a good piano, Kid? I tell you it IS a good piano! It took six men two hours to get it up here! Why, do you realize how much that thing WEIGHS?!"

It was clear there was no future in that job. I quit and left.

The owners of Pappy's Pub in Lapeer, Michigan have no idea how much their piano weighs, nor do they care.
Photo by Bob Milne, 1992

DO YOU WORK HERE?

Charley's Crab is perhaps the most elegant dining establishment in the entire southern-Michigan area. Its main dining room consists of a huge, cathedral-ceilinged room removed from a twenties-era mansion that overlooked Lake St. Clair before it was dismantled for some apartment project. The grand piano (underneath a huge hanging anchor) is in the bar area, immediately adjacent to this room.

During the years I played at 'The Crab,' management had little newspapers sitting around in the bar describing the premises, food, and the piano players, who were myself and Bob Seeley. It contained brief synopses on both of us, including the fact that I composed rags.

A little learning must be a dangerous thing, because people would read these things, get interested, and then ask us all kinds of questions that no one would ever walk up to a perfect stranger and ask. It would go something like this:

"Hi! Do you write rags? Oh, how nice! Where do you live? Really? Are you married? What does your wife do? When do you practice? And what do you do when you're not playing the piano?"

I finally began answering that question with:

"I play ragtime, madam. And when I'm not playing ragtime, I am THINKING about ragtime."

But then there was the classic question that, believe it or not, I've been asked more than anything else:

"Excuse me, sir, but do you have a job?"

One night I was in a dour mood. I don't usually do stuff like this, but I was sick and tired of endlessly inane questions this time. Therefore, when some woman with a bozo-esque date started asking me where I lived, etc., I told them basically this:

"Hello. I'm glad you asked. You see, the owners of this company are very nice people, and when they moved their offices out of the basement, they said I could fix up a room at one end and move in."

(Charley's Crab, of course, doesn't have a basement.) I continued:

"I do most of my rag writing in the small hours of the morning when I'm through cleaning the kitchen and have the prep work done for tomorrow. Chef goes crazy if I don't have the chowder just the way he wants it. The clams have to be diced just right."

(The place didn't even serve clam chowder either, but it was all I could think to say at the moment. Since they seemed to believe what I'd said so far, I bullshooted on.)

Charley's Crab, Troy, Michigan
Photo by Richard Berry, 1992

"They give me some time off from the kitchen at 4:00 P.M. to come out here and play the piano. I don't mind though, because otherwise they'd have to pay someone to do this."

(Can you imagine? PAY someone to play this thing? I decided to quit now while I was still ahead.)

"Well, thanks folks. I have to get back to the pastry oven. Did you like those rolls? Oh, thanks. I was afraid I had too much salt in them. See you next time, now. God bless."

The Journeyman Piano Player excused himself and left. To this day I truly believe that they thought I cleaned the kitchen at night, diced the clams in the morning, wrote rags in the basement like some kind of troll in a dungeon, and played the piano for the hell of it to help cut management costs. What has this business come to?

DON'T SHOOT THE PIANO PLAYER;
(Someone Already Did)
(Or if they didn't, they will shortly)

Walt Gower, the clarinetist with the Sweet Violets Ragtime Band, has proved many times that he can handle any situation.

One occasion in particular involved a certain piano player, who must remain nameless for soon to be seen obvious reasons. This pianist's, if I may warp the term slightly, style and manner are hard to describe. When he plays, he seems to feel that the faster he can get through whatever he's playing, the better he's played it. For some strange reason, he attacks the piano with both speed and volume as he seems to compete against some musical opponent in his mind. Consequently, chords have been known to be chaotic, wrong, and cluster-fudges of various notes that have nothing at all to do with each other. Interesting expressions have been noted on customers' faces during these performances.

The pianist in question suffered an unfortunate incident. A twist of fate placed him outside a party store when hoods robbed it, and he was hit by several bullets during their escape. Our pianist was taken to the hospital with superficial gunshot wounds. Not to worry. None of them were life-threatening. Just bed and rest and he'd be fine in a week or so.

When I learned of this, I relayed the story to the band during a break at a yacht club. When I mentioned that he'd been shot, Gower didn't wait to find out if he was dead or alive, but rather countered with:

"Shot three times, eh? He must have been playing the piano and somebody RECOGNIZED THE TUNE!"

Sweet Violets with Duke Heitger, cornet
Photo by Joanne Domka, 1991

AND THE BAND PLAYED ON...

Professional piano players are always having to combine music with show business in order to keep the attention of large parts of typical audiences. This can take the form of relating some historical anecdote to the music, letting some clown from the audience sing, or perhaps staging some sort of outrageous comic relief for the fine diners.

One of the comic reliefs that has helped me survive too many years in this business is one developed at the Dakota Inn Rathskeller, where the piano is prominently displayed on a small stage. It worked this way:

Using some hackneyed tune such as Five Foot Two, the Journeyman Piano Player would commence playing faster and faster, adding such theatrics as an occasional elbow smash in the bass or a foot on the high notes.

Piano at the Dakota Inn
Photo by Richard Berry, 1992

Crowds love this kind of thing, and during the course of one of these performances, I would ease myself toward the edge of the piano bench, gradually working the piano-theatrics into a blur of meaningless sounds and sights until reaching the edge of the bench. Then - WHAM! The journeyman would crash from the bench underneath the piano, sending billows of dust flying into the air with the demise. Little hands and fingers would still cling to the keys as customers came to their feet in horror. Then, crawling around to look over the capsized bench, I'd yell:

"I'm sorry! I'm terribly sorry! I must have gotten carried away!"

I would then put the bench back up and finish the tune in a much subdued style now, as customers and owner alike chuckled over the stunt. Falling off the piano bench became a trademark at this location and, over years of repeated crashings, many customers actually requested it. We all got a good laugh out of it.

One night the band was at the Woodbridge Tavern, down by the riverfront. Nothing we did seemed to work on this particular occasion, and the band's attitude was starting to suffer. We'd played all the Dixieland favorites to polite applause and were now taking solos on 'Sweet Georgia Brown.' Clarinetist Walt Gower's usually upbeat outlook had degenerated to outright contempt as we tried to entertain the non-entertainable. Finally, Gower grunted something or other to indicate that I take a few solos on this tune.

The first time through, I didn't stray far from the melody. The second time, there was some added rhythm in the bass. Getting into it now, the journeyman got carried away and was roaring through it a third time when all hell broke loose. Somehow, and to this day I don't know how, the piano bench broke in half. It had always been a piece of garbage (the legs were always coming loose, the cross-support was always coming unglued), but this time I looked up to see the piano going UP (meaning I was going DOWN) and the floor was going to be my next stop. I grabbed the keyboard with both hands out of instinct, and when the dust settled a familiar scene was present; little hands and fingers were still clutching the keys while a demolished bench rolled in pieces on the floor.

The audience went wild. They thought it was great.

The band went wild. They thought it stunk, and wondered why I had reached to this bottom-of-the-barrel stunt to further desecrate what was already a difficult night for us. But there was more.

Gower, sitting atop his bar stool with clarinet in hand, was glaring down at me unamused. As I gazed up from the rubble he yelled:

"Milne! You idiot! What the hell do you think you're doing?! Leave that cheesy trick at home when you come on jobs with us! Now, get your ass up here and finish your solo!".

A customer handed me a rail-back chair, I kicked the demolished bench out of the way, finished the solo and the band played on.

I've often wondered; does life imitate art, or does art imitate life? What goes around comes around, I guess. Or is 'what goes up also comes down' more appropriate? Somebody help me on this one.

Ode To The Barroom

The banjo lay busted in two,
The piano was tusked, through and through;
Our agent, the clown,
Wrote the wrong address down,
And the band played a gig at the zoo

They wore chartreuse and orange and grape,
From their cages, we had no escape
And when we played 'Jungle Town'
It brought the house down
As they screeched, howled, roared, and went ape.

Tom Saunders, tuba, & Ned Spencer, banjo with the Sweet Violets
Photo courtesy of Wally Lubzik, circa 1980

SINGING THE GAMUT

O.K. gang. Here's your etymology lesson for today. By the time you finish reading this, you should be familiar with what 'etymology' means, and can maybe add a study of it to your New Year's resolutions.

How many of you know the origin of the word 'gamut?' Have you ever heard anyone use the term 'run the gamut' or (incorrectly) 'run the gambit?'

The word 'gamut' comes from a musical derivation. Back in the days of Bach and before, it was common for church choirs to sing in what is called 'solfeggio.' Solfeggio means 'the application of the sol-fa terms to singing.' In other words, rather than sing 'You are my sunshine,' you'd sing *'Sol-do-re-mi-mi'* in absence of having any words to sing.

However, during the Renaissance era, when solfeggio was invented, the scale was sung *'ut-re-mi-fa-sol-la-ut,'* rather than *'do-re-mi-etc.'* (Did you notice I left out the 7th tone 'ti?' You didn't? Well, I did, but the reason I omitted it is too lengthy to include here.)

'Do' replaced 'Ut' in relatively recent times. Crossword workers still find 'ut' to be the answer to 'Guido's low note.'

The lowest note to be sung by the choir was a low C in the bass, and since C's were sung as 'Ut,' the low C was known as the 'Gam Ut.' Anyone who could sing the entire range from low C to high C was said to be able to 'sing the gamut,' hence our present-day term that now applies to other things besides singing.

A couple other interesting words come from the old Gam Ut. So many church hymns ended, in the major keys, with the notes D-G-C that the solfeggio singers coined the phrase re-sol-ut as meaning the ending of something. Of course, our present term 'resolution' snuck into our language via this slang term back in the mid-to-late Middle Ages by those who retreated to taverns following rehearsals and quaffed to the re-sol-ut.

Their major key slang was good enough to sneak into our language unnoticed. I also snuck it into the first paragraph of this column, but there's more. I'm sitting here wondering how many of you noticed a minor key solfeggio-derived word that snuck into the first paragraph as well. Think you can find it?

(Was that too much of a hint? Should I have said 'somewhere on this page?' Oh, well. Too late now.)

GHOST PIANOS IN THE SKY

A friend once gave me a piano free of charge, on the condition that I move it from his apartment which he was vacating for warmer climes. It was a full upright, painted garden green, and weighed somewhere in the area of 400 stone, which included the pasted on Playboy centerfolds on the ends. It was sitting at the top of a long, narrow staircase that entered onto Main Street of Rochester, Michigan right next to the old Hills Theater and across the street from the pool hall.

My friend had moved it into the hallway because his rent had expired and the next tenant had by now moved in. As I stood there studying the monstrosity and trying to figure out how to get it down the stairs, the new tenant opened the door and said in a not-too-subtle way:

"When ya' going to get that thing out of here?"

"Soon," I answered. *"Soon."*

As time went on, I found that the task of getting that thing down a long, narrow flight of stairs was more than I bargained for, and yet every time I bumped into the new tenant, whether on the street or at the top of the stairs, he was all over me to get the piano moved. The dialogue was getting out of hand, too. Each encounter with him was more direct in his assessment of both me and the piano, and each time I could only answer with:

"Soon. I'll move it soon."

One night, returning from playing a job in Detroit, I stopped in the local bistro just five doors north of the theatre and the aforementioned piano. As I sat in the waning hours of legal bar-time trying to come up with a way to get the piano moved, an old man came wobbling through the door. He ordered a boilermaker, downed the whiskey, soothed his throat with the beer, and then said to the bartender:

"Harry, you won't believe what I saw tonight."

"What's that?" replied the easy-going bartender.

Another slug of beer, and then the man went on with:

"Well, I was on my way down here earlier, comin' down Main Street by the theatre, when suddenly I heard the goddamnedest noise I ever heard in my life. I stopped in my tracks, lookin' around to see where it was comin' from, and suddenly the door next to the theatre came crashing down and this piano come thunderin' out over the top of it. Why, it went sailin' right out over the curb and into the street

before it stopped."

The bartender, obviously not believing a word of it, looked up and said limply:

"Ya' don't say?"

Silence followed. As I was grabbing my things and preparing to leave town for a long time, the old man added:

"Why, when I saw that, I figured I was drunk and shouldn't probably be comin' here."

"So what'd you do?" asked the bartender, still humoring the old man.

"I turned around and went down to Pat Knapp's to drink it off," he replied.

Fearing that someone was going to figure some way to stick me with some kind of repair bill somehow, I didn't show my face in town for the next six months.

'OH, DANNY BOY'

Although I grew up in Rochester, Michigan, I went to college as a French horn major at the Eastman School of Music in Rochester, New York back in the late 50's. A lot of crazy things happened that were related to either stress of performance or a myriad of other achievement-related topics. One of these was the night that Jim Stuart sang 'Danny Boy' at the Town & Country Lounge.

Stuart was a fantastic lyric tenor. He is likely the best singer I have ever heard in my life, and on the night in question, both he and I had performed in a concert at the Eastman Theatre. We were wearing tuxedos, as I had been in the orchestra and he had been on stage as a soloist in some oratorio. Following the performance, we both went across the street to the Town & Country Lounge, a fine supper club and a favorite hangout for Eastman students.

The 'T. & C.' had an eight-foot grand piano, and on this night a huge metal vase of flowers swept up from its magnificent lid, a grandiose decoration that was both beautiful and noticeable. Stuart, however, hardly noticed it. He was downing one drink after another to relieve the anxiety left over from the performance. Gin gimlets, as I recall.

Finally, after I had lost count of what had passed before and thus into him, he asked me if I would play 'Danny Boy' on the piano so he could sing it. I agreed.

Stuart, resplendent in tails and tux, took his place in the crook of the piano, leaning on it somewhat to steady himself as I played the opening strains. Customers at tables looked up and smiled.

As he began, it was immediately obvious to everyone that he was a master. Everyone in the place stopped to listen as he sang the first verse with chilling beauty. Singing in the key of 'G,' the approaching high 'B' had the entire place wondering if he would be able to hit it. Stuart not only hit it, he graced it with such soft and lyric quality that shivers overcame all within. There was stunned silence as he ended the first verse and I played a few chords to steer him into the second.

Stuart was now in full concentration. He was singing with his eyes closed, and the silken quality of his voice was unbelievable. The phrases, enunciation, and lyric quality had them on the edges of their seats, and Stuart was now approaching the high note again. It was then that the booze caught up with him.

Suddenly, to everyone's horror, Stuart lurched to the side. He had momentarily lost his balance and his arm swung out now to steady himself. But it was a disaster. Instead of catching onto something to hold, he hit the metal vase of flowers. As I stared in amazement, the vase swayed first to the left, then to the right, and then rolled on its base to tilt ominously in my direction. And now, as the thing began to lean past the point of no return, I looked to see that Stuart was going to be of no use either. He was clawing madly at the side of the piano to keep his balance. The vase reeled once more and then came crashing down to empty its guts into the Steinway grand, and Stuart simultaneously went crashing down the side of the piano to the floor, disappearing with an ungodly 'thud.'

The next thing I remember is hands. Lots of them. Hands on my shoulders. Hands on my tux. The hands of cooks and waiters were all over us as they trundled Stuart and myself unceremoniously past the stunned diners and pitched both of us out the door.

I distinctly remember sitting on the curb, dressed in tuxedo, and listening as Stuart sobbed:

"I'm sorry, Bob. I'm really sorry!"

A cab eventually came along and picked us up. I should be thankful, I suppose, that it wasn't the police. Maybe they were on their way. Maybe, after all, it was a modern-day miracle that the cab got there first.

A GIG TO FORGET
(Call You 'Forgettable')

Some jobs are better than others, and the worst one I ever had was in one of the ritziest places in town, out there in Birmingham-Bloomfield. I'm not being too specific for what will become obvious reasons.

The clientele in this joint wore $1200.00 suits, $300.00 shoes, and thought that manners were short for man-hole covers. The management paid the lowest money in town, demanded the longest hours in the county, and blew their noses into the piano player's face so as not to offend the customers. And speaking of noses, you could count the hairs in the owner's as he continually looked down it at you. To play the piano in this joint was as stomach churning as the rides at Cedar Point.

And, yes, the piano. Polite words and the threat of being disenfranchised by the publisher of this sheet prevent me from describing it. But I'll try.

First, it was a spinet. Spinets are for people who want to make the payments on a piano without the bother of actually owning one. The shortness of their strings insures that every time the temperature changes, so does the tuning of the piano.

Second, despite its God-given handicaps, it was in abhorrent disarray besides. Plastic-covered keys were burned from cigarettes, a rug had been nailed across the back of it to guarantee that any sound that tried to escape was throttled beyond recognition, and the action warranted a sign permanently proclaiming "Chopin wept here."

Enough. Suffice it to be said that I couldn't stand the job, but at the time, I couldn't afford to be without it. So I played it.

One night as I sat playing a one-fingered rendition of 'Misty' to some maven's torrid delight, (the manager had come by yet again to tell me to *"hold it down, will ya?"*), I just couldn't take it any more. I had to get out of there. The trick was to get up and walk out without burning the bridge behind me, so I thought for a while to try to come up with a worthy excuse to leave but still be able to come back the next night. Finally, I came up with a plan.

I went to the phone and called a lady that I knew, telling her what I had in mind. She agreed that it should work. I returned to the piano, and was now playing *"Just a Closer Walk With Thee"* while some drunken sot informed me how *"all the blacks in New Orleans really get down on this one."* As I gritted my teeth and smiled (try doing that convincingly some time) the manager suddenly came running from the front desk to inform me:

"Bob! Bonnie just called! She says she's having the baby, and JOHN'S NOT HOME!

"OH-MY-GOD!" I yelled, jumping up from the keys in mid-chord and fleeing out the door, leaving the maven, sot, and manager behind. My car engine and squealing tires as I blew out of the parking lot never sounded so good.

The scam worked, but the job was so putrid that I had to quit about three weeks later.

Every time I see this place looming in the windshield, I remember Chuck Moss' immortal words when the band was playing in a different but similar ritzy joint. After some disgusting scene on the dance floor, during which the band had to watch a drunken debutante's overt sexuality, Moss put down his trombone long enough to say:

"Well, I guess that all the money in the world can't buy class."

THE ENVELOPE, PLEASE!

I was playing ragtime at Charley's Crab one evening in the late 70's. The bar was full with the after-work crowd and the grand piano behind the bar was surrounded also. The balcony, stretching along over my left shoulder, was filled with partiers as well, and occasional boisterous shouts would sift down every now and then. As the evening progressed, the yahooing from the balcony increased, and I would periodically cast a glance up there to see what was going on, but to no avail.

Finally, as I was going into the mid-section of the Pineapple Rag, I became aware of someone yelling *"STOP THE MUSIC! STOP THE MUSIC!"* The tones of his voice were so frantic that I actually did stop playing and turn with everyone else to see what was going on. We looked up at the balcony where some wild-eyed character was hanging halfway over the rail with a bunch of papers in his hands and yelling:

"I HAVE THE PAPERS!! THEY'RE FINAL!! THEY'RE FINAL!!"

He was grinning and waving them in the air as the customers, realizing what was happening, burst into smiles and began applauding. But now he was yelling even louder:

"AREN'T THEY BEAUTIFUL? THE PAPERS! AREN'T THEY BEAUTIFUL?"

The customers were hoisting their glasses in salutes as he was now searching for something contained in the papers. Pointing at what appeared to be a judge's signature, he yelled:

"SHE'S GONE!! SHE'S GONE!! THANK GOD AND GREYHOUND SHE'S GONE!!"

The customers were applauding wildly now when suddenly:

"DO YOU WANT TO SEE THEM? I'LL SHOW THEM TO YOU! I'LL SHOW THEM TO YOU!"

He took off running through the balcony to get downstairs as fast as he could.

Once in the bar, he handed the papers to all kinds of people for their examination and approval. They were patting him on the back, buying him drinks (and he was downing them on the spot), and men and women alike were giving him warm hugs as he shared his ecstasy with all. At times, a perusing customer would mumble 'Hmm...,' raise his hand for silence, then read from the papers in stentorian tones:

"And the court shall decree that the house and all furnishings shall

go to the plaintiff, Mr. such-and-such."

The place would then burst into wild screaming and yelling as he accepted congratulations all over again, his friends in the balcony even leaning over the rail to give their blessings to the proceedings going on below. Someone else would read from another paragraph:

"The request for alimony is denied..."

More tumultuous applause would erupt as the most intimate of details of the divorce papers were shared with the drinking clientele at Charley's Crab.

A lady eventually came down from the balcony with a section of the celebration cake, and they shared it with all of us. At one point, between munches, the whole place hoisted drinks in the air to sing:

"THERE GOES THE BRIDE..."

Probably everyone in the restaurant read the papers before he finally drifted off to rejoin his group. But the singing followed him:

"I HAD SOMEONE ELSE BEFORE I HAD YOU..."

He'd lean over the railing above to express his approval. Then, a few minutes later the bar would be singing:

"SO LONG, IT'S BEEN GOOD TO KNOW YA'..."

He'd blow kisses to us down below.

I wonder if the 'ex' was having a similar bash? Anybody know? What are they singing as we speak? Is it printable? How can we get a copy of it? Out with it, darn you! Inquiring minds want to know...!

A NIGHT IN DRAG

It was Halloween at the Sundog Restaurant, where I played for three years in the early 70's, and all employees were asked to arrive in costume. I called up my old friend Harry Schemer to see if he'd go along with the gag I had in mind. His answer was affirmative, so on Halloween night Mr. & Mrs. Harry Schemer arrived, arm in arm, at the Sundog for dinner next to the piano. I, in drag, was Mrs. Harry Schemer.

The long blond wig, the large round glasses, the non-descript pantsuit, and the bulging white turtle-neck sweater was all it took to fool every one of the waitresses and customers that I had come to know in the place. We walked right through them all as the hostess seated us at our reserved table next to the piano. She even lit the little candle for us.

"Where's your piano player tonight?" asked Harry of the hostess. *"We hear that he's excellent and have come all the way across town to hear him."*

Casting a glance at the empty piano, she quickly replied:
"He'll be right here, sir."
Harry, checking his watch, replied:
"Very well, then. We'll wait."

After the salads were served, and after I should have started playing half an hour ago, Harry called for the manager.

"Excuse me, sir," he began, *"but just where the hell is your piano player tonight? The food here is O.K., if you don't mind, but we really came to hear your piano player. Where IS HE?"*

The manager mumbled some words about *"he'll be right along, sir. I apologize for the delay,"* and hurried away. Over the next half hour, Harry repeatedly called over all the assistant managers, the head waitress, the bartender, and even the busboy as he raised hell because the piano player wasn't there. I, hidden in the obscurity of company imposed costume, contentedly munched on New York steak and potatoes au gratin as Harry vented his rage loudly and in all directions:

"What kind of place is this? They have a piano, they advertise a pianist, we come all the way the hell across town to eat this crap..."

Following dinner, Harry sat there fuming. But then, he suddenly cast a capricious glance at our waitress and asked her (out of my earshot) if she had anything special for anniversaries. Eager to please the 'furious customer,' she immediately ran off and returned with a cake covered with candles. It was then that she, accompanied by every last waitress in the place, sang 'Happy Anniversary' to me and Harry Schemer. They even took a Polaroid picture of us as we sat with our arms around each other next to the piano, at the same time the managers were calling my house, frantically wondering where the hell I was.

After an hour and a half of eating steak, eating cake, screaming about the lack of a piano player, and after one of the waitresses had been hanging around because she 'felt something was strange,' suddenly the room was filled with the cry of *"OH YOU LITTLE BASTARD!"* when she finally realized what was happening right there in the middle of the restaurant. I was attacked en mass by the waitresses who tried to put the anniversary cake over my head at the same time the manager was running into the room yelling:

"In drag? What do you mean 'in drag?'"

Harry pretended outrage at their behavior. He ranted and raved as he insisted they leave me alone:

"WHAT? TAKE YOUR HANDS OFF MY WIFE! WHAT ARE YOU DOING? I'LL SUE THIS PLACE...!"

I finished the night behind the piano as Mrs. Harry Schemer, and when the company vice president came in and sat next to me at the piano bar, it took fifteen minutes before the man who hired me for the job realized it was me. Squinting through his glasses at me with a puzzled expression, he queried:

"Bob? Is that you in there? Bob; what the hell are you doing?"

It was the first and last time I ever did anything like this. Do not look for a repeat performance of this one.

CALLING MRS. MALAPROP

Strange things occur in the English language. People hear something said, but it's either a new term to them and they misunderstand the phonetics, or they turn it around in their brain somehow to fit already existing sounds. How else, oh wise ones, can we explain the number of times I've received a request to play the 'Make Believe Rag'?

I, too, was confused when this first happened, but I've received that particular request both spoken and written. The first time was strange. It kind of 'weirded me out,' so to speak. Here was a grown, adult male standing in front of me, and with a straight face he was asking me to play the 'Make Believe Rag.' When I finally figured out that he meant 'Maple Leaf Rag,' I exercised self-control to keep from laughing, for the man simply didn't know any different. Then, spread over the following years, I would periodically receive a written request (usually on a bar napkin) with the scribbled words 'Make Believe Rag' on it. A Journeyman, of course, simply plays the request and, if the opportunity presents itself, politely informs the listener of their error. He also informs them of their misunderstanding of the composer's name:

"Oh, hi there! Thank you for asking for the Maple Leaf Rag! Since I grew up in Canada, that tune has special meaning to me!"

(I didn't grow up in Canada, but this gets these people thinking in similes, which helps solve the problem.)

"Uh," begins their likely response, *"yes, er - I like that tune, too. Didn't Scott Johnson write it?"*

(No, I'm not making this up. People have said 'Scott Johnson' to me many times.)

"Yes, he did," I always reply. *"Scott **JOPLIN** was a major figure in the ragtime movement around the turn of the century."*

The only time I had zero luck with this topic was when some female hippy, back around 1979, asked me to play 'The Maple Leaf Rag.' When I finished, she said:

"Man, she was a hell of composer."

Puzzled, I kind of mumbled something about 'Scott Joplin from Missouri.' The response I elicited, however, was wild. This woman's eyes suddenly flashed and she informed me, in no uncertain terms, that the 'Maple Leaf Rag' had been written by **JANIS** Joplin, the cult-hero of the rebellion set. All attempts on my part to set her straight only served to fuel her ire. This woman had somehow built up Janis Joplin's abilities to include the writing of piano rags, and any information to the contrary from 'know-nothing entertainers who cater to the establishment' was simply not what she wanted to hear. Since no one ever wins an argument with a customer, I took an hour-long break and ate dinner.

Malaprops come in all sizes and shapes. I have been asked, on the proverbial bar napkin, to play 'Pine Top's Myth.' (For the sake of anyone not familiar with this 1920's era boogie-woogie player, Clarence Smith's nickname was 'Pine Top' Smith).

I clearly remember being handed a request, in Charley's Crab, to play **'Blew By You.'** Trying to keep a straight face, I looked up to see a middle-aged lady standing there with a somber expression:

"Can you play it?" she asked rather directly.

"Uh, yes," I replied, then went into the old classic by Roy Orbison, **'Blue Bayou.'**

Another one that happened in Charley's Crab involved the decor. The Crab is a seafood restaurant, and the decorations are, naturally, nautical. Paintings of ships hang on the walls, dory oars hang from the rafters, ship's compasses sit around, and everywhere you look reflects the seafaring nature of the place.

One night, a couple characters came in from the hotel next door and plunked themselves down on barstools next to me. I greeted them politely and continued playing ragtime. They were up to something, I could tell, because they had mischievous smirks on their faces and kept glancing around at everyone. They eyed the waitresses, the customers, and even got up to view the people in the dining room once. Finally, they came back to me, saying:

"Well, where are they?"

"Where are what?" I asked.

They smirked to each other and glanced around again. Then:

"Where's all the whores?"

I turned and looked down the bar in back of me at our distinguished clientele. I recognized most of them as regular customers, yet here were a couple of clowns wondering 'where's all the whores.' Finally, I said:

"I think I'm missing something, gentlemen. There are no whores in here."

But their response was adamant:

"*That's not what we heard, buddy. We were told to just go sit near the piano player and we'd see them.*"

After a momentary pause, during which time I contemplated everything from creation to predestination and time, I asked:

"*What the hell are you talking about?*"

"*A guy in the hotel bar,*" they replied. "*He said the place was full of whores. He said to sit by the piano player and we'd see them 'swinging from the rafters.'*"

The Journeyman Piano Player slowly looked up at the dory oars, 'swinging from the rafters,' just as slowly closed the cover to the keys, and once again left to take a break. There's a limit to how much of this stuff I can take.

Another malaprop involves my name, Milne. The 'e' at the end is silent, and 'Milne' rhymes with 'kiln.' My father is from northeastern Scotland (Aberdeenshire), where 'Milne' means 'a mill,' and is pronounced 'Mehl.' At any rate, the American people pronounce the 'e.' Hence, 'Mil-NEE.'

I am used to this, so it doesn't bother me. Certain Milne families in this country actually 'went with the flow' and incorporated the new pronunciation into their names, thus becoming 'Mil-NEEs.' But what is amazing is this recreation of a typical conversation that I've been through more times than I can count:

"*Hello. Are you Bob Mil-NEE?*"

"*Uh, Milne, yes.*"

"*Oh? I'm looking for Bob Mil-NEE?*"

"*Well, we pronounce it 'Milne.'*"

"*Will you spell that, please?*"

"***M-I-L-N-E.***"

Pause. Then:

"*Isn't that pronounced* ***'Mil-NEE?'***"

Hello? Hello? Is anybody home?

THE CLUB BERKLEY

In the early 1970's, the Club Berkley still held forth on Woodward Avenue. Its glory days were behind it, but the place could still put on a good dinner and dance trio on the weekend. During the week, a single piano player would tinkle the keys for the dining enjoyment.

I had finished my job early one night and drove some twenty miles cross-town to hear my friend Elliot playing solo at the club. He, like so many of us in this business, had to slog through the endless requests for 'Alley Cat' and various other imbecilic tunes that somehow or other represented music to someone paying the freight. This night was no different. Elliot grimaced to himself when he saw me come in, and he tried to put a quick finish to the tune. Sad, but all of us in this business have to play garbage at times in order to get paid at the end of the week.

Finally taking a break, he grabbed me by the arm and hustled me over to the bar.

"I need one," he explained, as the bartender immediately set down a straight gin for him. Elliot introduced me to the bartender, adding 'without whom I could not survive a single night in this place.' I understood, of course, and now the bartender laughed as he related stories of his own pressured existence trying to earn a living. While we talked, a strictly-business-type manager came by to ask my friend:

"How long ya' gonna' be on break?"

"Just a few more minutes," he replied, even though his break had hardly begun. The chalk-faced manager grunted and moved on.

Both Elliot and the bartender invited me to play for a while. I could see that my friend needed a long break, the manager didn't care who played as long as the matrons at the tables were happy, and I also thought it might lead to future business. I agreed.

Elliot sat at the piano bar with me. I was careful to play slow tunes without much embellishment. This causes drunks to think that they could do as well as the guy playing the chords and avoids the pitfall of jealousy from local heroes. They liked what I was doing. A woman even waved with her pinky as she held her drink to indicate approval. Elliot had swilled down another gin by now, and I was beginning to wonder if I'd have to finish the night for him. Oh well; only had two hours to go. He had done me a lot of favors before so if needed, I could do this one for him. I played on, but suddenly there was chaos over at the bar.

I turned to see what was wrong. Elliot, the poor devil, was too out of it to notice the commotion and just kept sucking up what was between the ice cubes. Someone by the bar was yelling about an ambulance, and so many people were running around in confusion that I quit playing to go back and see what had happened. Elliot followed me.

When we reached the bar, the bartender was flat on his back. He'd had a heart attack. Customers were picking him up and now carried him over near the front entranceway where they yelled in frustration over the non-arrival of the ambulance yet. I could see that the bartender was turning blue, and sadly realized that the ambulance was too late the instant he'd hit the floor. But now, someone was tugging on my arm.

"Hey, uh, whatever your name is; would you start playing again? Something bouncy? Try and liven this place up? Get people's minds off this?"

It was the manager. And as I stared in disbelief at him, his tone escalated aggressively:

"Come on; get over there! We'll take care of this!"

If I ever have to make a nomination for the most callous slob I've ever run into, this guy is it. The Club Berkley closed and was demolished about ten years after this scene. It's gone, but unfortunately the memory of that jerk will live forever.

THE JOURNEYMAN PIANO PLAYER

The professional pianist has got to be a lot of different things. He has to be a psychologist, psychiatrist, peace-maker, consoler, psychic, and any number of other unorthodox guises in order to get through the night and ultimately get paid. A place I played in about twenty years ago had so many lover's arguments, so many dates with other people's wives, and so many alcohol induced confessions better suited for the National Enquirer that I was finally forced to hang up a sign that read:

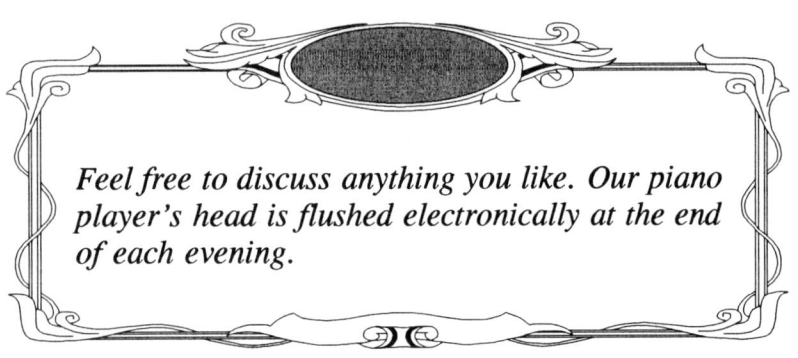

Feel free to discuss anything you like. Our piano player's head is flushed electronically at the end of each evening.

Dodging faux pas and trying to cover for screw-ups is a way of life for any Journeyman Piano Player. For instance, I was playing an upright piano one night in a downtown 'supper club,' if you'll accept that description, and was working some tune or other into a fifteen-fingered rendition using every part of the piano at once. Sometimes this works and sometimes it doesn't, but the point is that it seemed to be working this time, so consequently the dining patronage were watching me closely.

The lamp sitting atop the piano to my left was casting an eerie glow on all of this, as well as the candle-in-a-bottle rocking along at the right hand end of the keys. Both shook from the vibrations emanating forth.

As I continued working up this number, I suddenly became aware that a gigantic roach was lethargically crawling along the top of the piano, periodically stopping to sit up, wave its antennae around like semaphore flags, and then continue lurching along in the direction of the lamp.

Was I sick? Was I disgusted? Was I nauseated?

Nah! The journeyman has to be equal to the occasion and prevent the sight from reaching sandwich-munchers at tableside, who would soon see the Luke-Skywalkerish thing lurching toward the lamp.

The Journeyman Piano Player certainly cannot swat it. Its juices might splatter, sending paying customers puking from their tables, never to return.

The Journeyman Piano Player can not brush the creature away, for then the paying customers would see it racing across the floor as it escaped, thereby causing them to go racing across the floor as they turned into non-paying customers escaping out the door.

No. The Journeyman Piano Player winks at the audience as he plays, picks up the candle-in-a-bottle with the right hand, and dumps the melted wax over the antennae-waving roach, resulting in a cavalcade of hot wax pouring down onto the keys while the left hand strides on in time.

The audience, of course, thinks this is hilarious. Since they weren't aware of the roach, they think this is a stunt by the journeyman to finish the tune without use of the center keys. They were right. It ended up with a Franz Liszt type ending, each hand at opposite ends of the keys to keep out of the wax, flailing away on the final chords as the octaves around middle C dripped down onto the journeyman's shoes.

The audience loved it. The applause was both sincere and heart-felt. The journeyman stood up, bowed, and sloshed away to repair the damage. The remaining three years of that job were played with an unusual wax formation high above middle C.

Madame Tussaud would have been proud. She never dreamed of the like.

Old Joe's Barroom
circa 1961

I had lunch at Old Joe's Barroom,
And there, you might surmise,
You couldn't tell if the bread was boiled
Or they served the grease to save the fries...

So I swept the garbage to the floor
And there, before their very eyes,
I pulled them buzzing from the soup
And lo, I ate the flies.

DODGING DISASTERS

A gentleman I had known for years had passed away, and the wake was being held in a local restaurant. The widow asked me if I would play the piano for a while, and although I wasn't in much of a mood to do so, I respected her wishes and obliged.

The music seemed to lift the dreary mood of the place, and many people were telling me how much they enjoyed it. I politely thanked them.

Sam, the local barber, came in the door. He had known the dear departed and had stopped by to give his condolences. After speaking with the widow for a moment, he sat down at the piano with me.

Everything was going smoothly. I was playing Sam's requests as well as anyone else's who stopped by, and now it was nearing the time to quit, but Sam had one more request.

I began playing it and he began softly singing the words, but after several strains had gone by, I suddenly realized that a horrendous blunder was taking place. Aghast, I looked up to see if anyone had noticed yet, and they hadn't. So I modulated out of Sam's request and into something completely different.

Sam looked at me totally puzzled, and I will never forget the look of horror on his face when I informed him that the dear departed was being cremated even as we played the request - SMOKE GETS IN YOUR EYES.

Hopefully, the Journeyman Piano Player had dodged yet another disaster of Gong Show proportions. We never found out, though. We were afraid to ask.

RANDY'S

The factory town of Flint, better known as 'Buick City' to the locals, lies about 60 miles north of Detroit. Use your intuition to determine what kind of piano playing they want at such establishments as the Rusty Nail. Keep in mind that the customers serve themselves while the bartender lies passed out on the  pool table. Don't worry; they're all honest enough to not take advantage of the poor bastard. And they play cards instead of pool until he wakes up.

Supper clubs around Flint have a peculiar aura about them. It's hard to describe, but the bulk of their business is transacted on the second and fourth Fridays of the month, both of which happen to coincide with paydays in the factories. One of these illustrious places, Randy's, phoned me about playing during their recently-begun cocktail hour. I had never heard of the place, but agreed to come over and meet the owner. So put yourself in the place of the journeyman and imagine that this is actually happening to you instead of me:

You are driving down a main street through Flint, clutching a scrap of paper in your hand as you search for the address. You find that buildings on both sides of the street advertise such things as 'Massage Specialists,' 'The World's Finest Adult Entertainment,' 'Tabletop dancers,' and 'Movies; Must have proof of age.' Cadillacs and Town Cars are parked in front of little buildings lacking signs of what their purpose is, and some woman in a leather mini-skirt is hitch-hiking her way home from, presumedly, the factory. Remembering that long hair is dangerous in the shops, you wonder why this voluptuous siren allows hers to hang down over her shoulders almost to her belt. After almost crashing into the car slowing down to pick her up, you finally come to a neon sign proclaiming 'Randy's Supper Club.'

You are greeted at the door by a host whose own shoulder-length hair still shows the ring mark from his recently undone pony-tail.

"You'se want a table?" he mutters.

You are now entering a room that cannot be described until your eyes adjust to the blackness. You say 'excuse me' to the seated guest you have just fallen over and now, picking yourself off the floor, you notice that the only light in the room comes from a bandstand off to the left. You see drums, keyboards on racks, three guitar stands, a poster of rockers made up to look like creatures from the dead, and a spinning ball up above all this which reflects droplets of light around the room as it turns.

Had enough yet? Want me to take over? Well, O.K., you're brave. Go ahead and continue on for a few moments pretending you're the Journeyman Piano Player. Just holler if you want me to take over.

You now find that your host is standing next to a table with a white table cloth on it. He doesn't say anything, but just indicates to you that this is where he wants you to sit. You guess that he didn't say anything because he is unfamiliar with such phrases as 'Your table, sir,' or 'I'm sure you will enjoy this spot, sir,' or something equally intelligent. You also guess that he is either too ignorant or unmannered, one or the other, to pull out a chair for your wife, so you do it. She sits down. When you sit down, you notice that there are actually two white table cloths, one on top of the other, which create a rather spongy surface to eat from.

"Why this?" you wonder, imagining what can be underneath which requires two table cloths to cover it up.

Seated now, nothing happens. Your eyes are gradually adjusting to the dark, and soon you see a long bar to one side. Three men are yukking it up with the barmaid. Two of them wear cheesy suits and the one in the center wears an open-at-the-top blue shirt. The barmaid - Great God, what's this...?

Suddenly a waitress is dumping menus on the table. She's gone before you can mutter even a word, so now you look back to the bar to confirm what you just saw and yes, the barmaid is NOT wearing a bra. She's not wearing a shirt, either. We've obviously arrived during the 'cocktail hour two-fer-one special' and the three men in front of her are having a great time. The term two-fer-one is taking on several diverse meanings at once in your spinning brain.

Still here? Well, O.K. Go ahead pretending for a while longer.

"What can I get choo' guys?"

The waitress is back. You order 'medallions,' whatever the hell they are. They were listed under the steak section, and your match burned out before you could read any more of the menu, so you order what you've already found.

Leaning back in your chair now, you try to relax and figure out what is in this place. You put your hands behind your head and stretch back in your seat, and it is then that you bump into some macabre thing in the darkness behind you. Turning around, you find yourself looking at some sort of wooden configuration that slowly rocks back and forth from your bumping into it. This apparition glows eerily in the sporadic light from the bandstand like some sort of phosphorescent mushroom rising up from the floor, and you stare at it for a moment or so until you're able to perceive a form. Slowly, it dawns on you what this thing is. It's the piano.

Your waitress is back with the salads, and you've eaten them without ever speaking a word. When she returns with your 'medallions,' (center-cut steaks, it turns out) you ask her if Randy is here. She says she'll get him for you and departs.

As you bite into your medallion, you see her saying something to the guy in the blue shirt at the bar, and he unplugs his eyes from the barmaid's boobs long enough to turn around and squint in your direction. Realizing that it takes a few moments for pupils to adjust (you have just been through this) you can understand his confused look as he, seated on a barstool with drink in hand, just stares blankly out into the blackness of the dining room. Finally, he smiles in your direction, arises and comes to your table. Congratulations. You have just met Randy.

Chickened out yet? O.K., go ahead and talk to him. You're the one who asked for this.

At the table, Randy seems unable to understand that you don't want a drink. When you euphemistically tell him 'I'm allergic to it,' he doesn't seem to readily grasp the meaning and, feeling inadequate in some way, he continues to insist that he buy you a drink. Having a Coke isn't good enough and he feels insulted that you won't have something from his lavish assortment of fine boozes behind the bar. Finally, using the out-and-out admission that you almost died from alcohol addiction and that it took a God-sent miracle to intervene, you seem to have gotten his attention somewhat. Confused now, he doesn't seem to know how to act or what to say, but finally:

"*Well, what do you think of my piano?*" he asks, scratching his head with one hand and gesturing to the glowing thing in back of you with the other. You recall to yourself a joke heard many years ago about a kid who was supposed to use the word 'beautiful' in a descriptive sentence. He stood up in class and announced:

"When I showed my report card to my father, Mrs. Jones, he said - 'Beautiful. Beautiful. Just fucking beautiful.'"

Therefore, you answer:

"*Beautiful, sir. Beautiful. Your piano is just beautiful.*"

Had enough? O.K., I can understand that. It's starting to get a little dicey in here, isn't it? Don't feel bad, though. I think you did pretty good to take it as long as you did. But I'll take over now so you can read the rest of this from the safety of your living room chair. From here on, go ahead and imagine that it's ME going through this rather than you because this, like everything else in this book, really happened to me.

Randy now explains that the guy who was playing for cocktail hour is the drummer with the band also, so he can't play both the early and late shifts.

"*He's REALLY GOOD!*" he tells me. "*Have you heard him?*"

I nod 'yes' and continue munching on the medallion (it's actually pretty good) recalling that I'm already familiar with this guy that he's talking about. Zoro, (not his real name) is a rock-band drummer who taught himself piano. Everyone in Flint thinks this guy is fantastic, and I recall to myself sitting around a piano bar somewhere else last month with Zoro's mother seated at the other end informing the clientele how good her son was.

I noticed, at the time, that he knew perhaps five chords in three keys, could do thumb-runs like Jerry Lee Lewis, and could beat the shit out of the piano like nothing you'd ever heard before. When he'd finish beating the shit out of it in 'C', he'd quiet down, modulate into 'F', slowly start building up steam, and then beat the shit out of it in 'F' the same way he'd just finished beating the shit out of it in 'C.' Between tunes he was very pleasant and talkative, and every other sentence helped to reinforce the notion of how good he and his blow-dried hair were. People in Flint were impressed, and I ate through the medallions listening to Randy tell me how fantastic the legendary Zoro was.

With dinner finally over, Randy invited me to play the piano. I arose and immediately tripped over something at the bottom of it. Randy explained that the back casters had been broken off. Hence, there were two little blocks cut from a two-by-four holding up the back of the spinet piano and 'sometimes the buss-boys don't get them all the way under and they stick out a little. Sorry 'bout that.'

When I sat down on the piano bench, it swayed ominously. Being a Journeyman Piano Player and not wanting to call attention to the collapsing piece of garbage (and thus embarrassing the host) I used my foot to kick the legs into line. This stunt causes the dining patrons to wonder what's wrong with ME rather than what's wrong with the piano. And through the ever flickering lumens I could see that it must have worked. Randy was smiling as he sat at my table, drink in hand and blabbering away to my wife who was doing everything possible to ignore him.

I began to play something quiet and, after receiving stone silence, went into another tune. Glancing up to see Randy's reaction, I discovered he was gone. But not for long. Apparently bored with a female who didn't adulate all over him, I found him seated once again between his buddies at the bar, his back to me as the barmaid bounced up and down running drinks to customers.

After playing several different styles ranging from easy-listening to fast and involved, it became apparent that some crashing noises were coming from the bandstand. I turned to find that Zoro had come in while I was playing and was beating the drums on the stage. Figuring that this would cease in a moment, I ignored him and played another tune. But the drums gradually became louder and louder, and I realized that this character who had been Flint's golden boy for the last couple of years couldn't stand someone else actually playing the piano. I got the feeling that he'd never heard anything in the bass other than a repeated chord over and over, and could not condone a right hand that could play scale passages of more than three notes or arpeggios going beyond one octave. So now he banged on the drums louder and louder as he attempted to call attention to himself and away from me. Finally, I turned around and yelled across the room:

"DO YOU MIND?"

He looked up, as if surprised.

"DO YOU MIND SHUTTING UP UNTIL I'M DONE?" I yelled again.

"Oh," came his reply. *"I was only tuning up for tonight."*
Tuning up? Drums?

I played this job for about two months. During this time, the woman in the black mini-skirt (remember her?) met so many men for a drink at the bar and then departed with them that I became convinced she was the official tour guide for the city of Flint. The piano was so flimsy that at one time a front leg fell off during a tune. It collapsed and leaned forward on me until I had to support it with my own legs, and also until the busboys came and rescued me. Randy said he'd get it fixed for tomorrow, but of course it was me who had to stick the legs back in the next day. Since no glue was available, I soaked a bar napkin in water, fitted it inside the hole, and shoved the leg back in. It served to make the hole a little tighter.

The job continued in this rotten fashion until one day I walked in to find that the piano had been moved to a different location in the dining room. I finally found it in the dark, readjusted the piano bench to keep from collapsing, and started to play something soft for an opening number. The piano felt unsteady somehow. My second number was something a little more profound, a boogie perhaps. I hit the first chords with more amperage than the previous tune when suddenly the piano lurched backwards, tilting hideously. I instantly realized that it had slipped off its two-by-four blocks ('sometimes the busboys don't get them in far enough.' Remember?) and now I watched in horror as the thing crashed over onto its back in the middle of the dining room, narrowly missing a guy seated at his table. And now, the bar-napkinned leg sagged horizontally next to my knee at roughly a thirty-degree angle, its caster spinning wildly as it reeled out a metallic, whining noise for the astonished patron's gracious dining entertainment.

It was about a week later when Randy told me:

"Uh, Bob, we don't think the piano is drawing in enough business. How does this sound to you; would you be willing to play for half of what we're paying you now? Just try it for a while and see how it goes?"

So I had medallions for dinner that night. Then I picked up my paycheck from Randy, signed the tab for the medallions, left a tip for the waitress, and never went back to that stinking place again.

Randy's went broke and closed about a year later.

PLAY IT AGAIN, SAM - 1977

Rancid strings, rancid hammers,
Slow air moves quite smokey, and
Like a wounded denture hangs there
Middle "C" -

Does she really want to hear
"Peg O' My Heart" Again?
How does it start?
How does it end?
Do they hear the augmented
Variant on the mediant
Or does the lime water
That he's bought her
Give him a lock?

Does the syncopated canon,
Low in the bass, moanin'
Ride through the diminished,
Unfinished - oh, forget it;
Is it two o'clock - yet?

JUSTICE PREVAILS

For reasons quick to be apparent, this article won't give a clue as to where it took place.

I was playing solo piano at a, uh, supper club that had remained in Detroit long after the city had been given over to criminals. Not only was it dangerous to drive there (cinder blocks were a favorite to be thrown from overpasses) it was also dangerous to play there (gunfire could be heard in the surrounding area at any hour, day or night).

The club had a clientele of everyone from professional gamblers to city policemen (who mingled freely with each other; they were buddies), street winos to chauffeured aristocrats. Everyone came to this place for the intrigue.

The club had a serious problem. Dopers had moved into a house a few doors away and were breaking into the club on a regular basis to steal everything they could find. The owner, considered by none to be anything less than ferocious himself, had patiently helped the police in their efforts to apprehend these thugs, but to no avail. Somehow, the dopers always managed to elude them and strike when no one was expecting it. Finally, after months of attempts, the police got lucky and caught them in the act.

A trial would be held about nine months later and the judge, faced with no room in the jails for these bums, was forced to give them probation. The dopers were back on the street again, laughing and happy. On the same night, the club was broken into and robbed again. The whole process started over.

The owner was furious and the police were disgusted, although this is not uncommon in Detroit, for law enforcement is constantly watching criminals laugh at the people who play by the rules. The police work a dangerous job, and the criminals laugh at them. It happens day in and day out.

One night the police were in the club again. They, as well as the owner, were understandably bummed by the whole thing and drank copious quantities while they shared their disgust with each other. Eventually, someone came up with an idea. They looked at each other quizzically for a moment, put their hands together to form a pact of agreement, and proceeded to implement this quaint but chillingly effective remedy to the situation.

First, one of them called their buddies at the fire department to explain the situation.

"Go for it," was the answer he received.

Second, the police casually drove their cars to barricade strategic points along the incoming streets. No one was to enter for a few minutes.

Thirdly, men with guns went to the house, lit the wicks of their Molotov cocktails, and fired them through the windows. As the bombs hit the rugs and walls, the police down the streets carefully turned all traffic aside.

As the area became uncommonly quiet from lack of traffic, dopers could be seen inside the house as they furiously tried to douse the flames, but it was too late. The old wooden frame was heating up fast as gasoline burnt like the fires of hell. The flames were hitting the downstairs ceiling now as the dopers hurled pans of water at it. Someone called the fire department but, for some strange reason, the fire department hung up the phone.

Frantic dopers finally went fleeing into the street and away as the fire now roared up into the second floor, consuming the house and anything else that might be in its path. Silent eyes from parked cars followed their departure. When the fire went through the roof, another call was made to the fire department, this time by the police. They didn't want to burn down the surrounding houses.

When the fire department arrived, they protected the nearby residences with precision accuracy. The house of dopers gave a mighty lurch and collapsed within itself, and now the fire hoses turned what was left into a slurry of charcoal, burnt shingles, and stench. When it was finally doused, the fire chief declared 'smoking in bed' as the cause, and the firemen picked up their hoses and went home.

When the Journeyman Piano Player arrived at the club for his appointed gig the next evening, he was given a tour and description of what had happened by someone who knew every detail. And, back inside the club, a strange phenomenon took place:

They were celebrating justice by singing, screaming, and yelling. What was strange was that it felt good to be a part of it.

OF HAMMERS AND STEMWARE

It was Sunday afternoon and the Sweet Violets Ragtime Band was at its appointed gig down in the inner city. The joint we were playing in was pretty close to Tiger Stadium and the city was hot to build a new stadium near the present site. Therefore, a dive frequented by stevedores, gamblers, and ladies of the night during their off-hours hired the band on Sunday afternoons. The idea was to make the dive look like it was taking in a lot of money even though it wasn't, so when the stadium authority bought the land the owners would get a higher price. Neat, eh? Good job security, eh?

Well anyway, we'd start playing at two o'clock in the afternoon. The stage was a narrow thing on which the back legs of the piano chair came within one inch of falling off the edge. If the chair would edge backwards somehow, both it and the journeyman would take a high-dive onto a low floor. This ominous and ongoing situation gave rise to the clarinet player's frequent jibes, as the proximity of the bench to the edge drew constant stares from the customers:

"And now, ladies and gentlemen, playing the piano for you without the safety of a net, the fearless, the one-and-only..."

The Journeyman Piano Player, undaunted by this seeming obstacle, fearlessly began each Sunday walking around the alley behind the bar with a claw hammer until he found a junk pallet or pile of scrap boards. He'd extract a few nails from same and go back inside. Therefore, the 'overture,' if you will, to our gig was the sound of screeching nails first being ripped loose from alley boards:

'SCREeeyaahhHHH.....!'

Then as our fans, having driven down from the suburbs alit from their cars on the surrounding streets, they would hear the journeyman at work inside:

"WHAM! WHAM! 'OW, GODDAMMIT!' WHAM! WHAM!"

The sound of nails being pounded into the stage (to prevent the chair from inching backwards any further) was a weekly occurrence. Number six box nails seemed to work the best; the chair legs had holes in the bottoms which fit neatly over said nails, securing the chair firmly in front of the piano. The only drawback was if we wanted to center the chair to the piano any differently, we had to push the piano one way or the other. The chair wouldn't move.

Once inside, our guests would find sticky table-tops left over from the previous night's binging, but our more seasoned fans would prove that they were equal to the occasion: they brought their own table cloths. They also brought their own glasses to drink from (they particularly enjoyed stem-ware) and seat covers to sit on so they didn't ruin their clothes. As time went on, they were actually bringing little vases of dainty flowers as a 'je n' sais quoi' to their tables.

On this one day in particular, a celebration of sorts was taking place at the bar as our guests arrived and set up. The stevedores were toasting and drinking; toasting and drinking. Louie, one of our favorites, was right in there with them. He had a hilarious routine which first required that he become shit-faced on boilermakers, and then he'd pick up an umbrella and strut slow-motion style through the joint. It was a classic that should have been filmed. But now, as the band members filtered in, the journeyman sat with some of the guests as we all observed this bacchanal going on at the bar. There was much laughing and hilarity. A birthday, perhaps? We didn't know, so every time they looked at us, we just smiled and looked back. They smiled, hoisted their drinks, and downed them.

The owner sat at the bar with them. In his early sixties, he was the only one in the place wearing a three-piece suit. He also had a fresh, deep scar on his forehead. We soon learned the purpose of the celebration; he'd been to one of Detroit's better chop houses the previous night when someone insulted his place. The owner came off his bar stool and attacked whoever the poor devil was who said it, and he finally landed an uppercut to the opponent's jaw that sent him flying on top of the hot hors d'oeuvres table. Following that, he simply sat down at the bar and continued drinking. This heart-warming and inspirational adventure in gracious dining is what they were celebrating with drinking and dialogue now:

"*Ya' knocked 'im right on top of the hot hors, did'ja?*"
"*Fuckin' - A.*"

The dive charged cover at the door. Someone always sat in a chair out on the street and collected three bucks from everyone who went in. Today, however, the guy that usually performed this duty was out of town. We knew he had to be out of town rather than in jail. If he'd been in jail, they'd be celebrating that, too. Anyway, someone had to be found to collect the cash. You guessed it: they chose Louie.

As we played throughout the afternoon, we would periodically gaze out the door and what we saw became repetitive; Louie was leaning back in the chair, hat pulled down to shade his eyes, and swilling from a beer bottle. Money was sticking out of all his pockets.

We noticed as one of the stevedores left and returned about twenty minutes later with a grocery bag full of booze. Apparently, the bar had run out of Canadian Club. We played on as we remembered that a licensed bar can only buy liquor from the state Liquor Control Commission, (the L.C.C.), and we kept quiet about the obvious purchase from the party store down the street.

"*They'll sneak the bag into the back,*" thought the journeyman, thinking that they'd slowly mix it in with their current stock. The journeyman was wrong. The stevedores set it down in the middle of the bar, unscrewed the tops, and swilled straight from the whiskey bottle before handing it to the barmaid to put the spout into. Looking away from this, the journeyman's eyes strayed out the door. Louie was tilted back in the chair finishing off another beer.

For some reason, a beer truck was parked near the side door to this place. As we played, we noticed the owner and the stevedores gradually moving toward the back of the bar to where the side door was, and we soon learned why. The beer truck had rolled up its side to expose case upon case of beer and these guys, including the owner, were partying on the street with the truck driver while we played on inside. The journeyman looked away from this in disbelief only to have his eyes pass across the door once again; Louie was tilted back in the chair, hat over his eyes, swilling beer.

Finally, it was six o'clock and we were done. Our band leader went to the owner to get paid. The owner went to Louie to collect the door money. Then we learned what had happened: Louie had bought so many rounds for his buddies with the door money that there wasn't enough cash left to pay the band. The truck driver, however, had 'In God We Trust' sticking out of his shirt pockets, and the barmaid had bountiful bankroll in her equally bountiful bra.

The Journeyman Piano Player stood outside in the hot summer sun as screaming thundered out the doors. It was all one-sided, coming from the owner, for Louie didn't have enough strength in his drunken body to argue back. Finally, the band leader came running out the door, shoved some money in my pocket, and said:

"*Bob; get the hell out of here!*"

About three weeks later when the band leader came back from an out-of-town trip to find the following message on his telephone answering machine:

"*Dan; the band is shit-canned. Call for details.*"

CAN YOU PLAY THE POLONAISE?

The professional piano player sometimes becomes subjected to the personal problems of various customers. I spent six years playing a five-night-a-week cocktail hour at a fashionable hotel, so learning how to deal with obtuse personalities becomes numero uno on the survival list. In short, 'deal, or wheel' (out the door). Would you like to take a shot at doing this? O.K.; you're on. I'll give you a situation and a multiple choice list of answers, and let's see how well you handle it.

SCENE ONE: Having just finished playing a foot-stomping boogie or rag (and received much applause), you now slow the tempo down for a change of pace. You're playing a blues when you notice some guy coming in from the lobby with two women, one on each arm. Without looking up, you:
   a) Hope that they sit at the three empty chairs at the piano, thus making the manager think that you're filling the piano bar.
   b) Hope he leaves the ladies at the piano bar, goes to the bar for some drinks, and someone else sits down on the third stool.
   c) Hope that they go anywhere in the place BUT the piano bar.
   d) None of the above.

Which one did you pick? My answer would have been 'C.' I'd want them anywhere else but where I was. Why? Well, here goes your psychology lesson for today.

To begin with, anytime you see some guy escorting two women, you know he's out to impress them both. Therefore, if he sits anywhere near you, you're going to be matching wits and quips with him. For instance, let's pretend that your wish did not come true and they're all sitting down around you now. The two ladies are looking at you with coy smirks while the guy snaps his fingers and yells *'WAITRESS!'* across the room, then turns to you, still snapping his fingers, and says:

"Hey piano player, snap it up a little, will ya?"
You:
   a) Tell him to screw-off. You just finished a snappy number before he came in the door.
   b) Look at him like he's weird. You've practiced squinting quizzically in the mirror for this.
   c) Suddenly sing the words 'Help me make it through the night' to whatever you're playing. Sing it several times in a row, no other words in between. People will get the idea.

d) Pretend you're deaf and dumb. If you do this, be prepared to bull-shoot your way past his and everyone else's next question: 'How do you play the piano?'

e) Smile and say, 'Yowsa,' boss.' Then continue playing exactly as you were until you're done.

Ready? Well, whatever answer you picked is correct. You see, the Journeyman Piano Player has given every one of those responses at one time or another. He's actually given a few that aren't print to fit, if you get the idea. You passed. We'll move on to the next one.

By now, the waitress has brought some drinks to them, he has ogled her body while the seated ladies continued smirking a la' in-crowd style, and you have now ended your tune and are trying to think of 'something snappy' to play for him. Noticing their 'snappy' clothes, ultra make-up, and blow-dried hair, you wonder which of the following to play:

a) New York, New York
b) New York, New York
c) New York, New York
d) New York, New York

Ready? Did you select Sonny Boy? (Forget it; that was a joke). O.K., I'll give you this one. You're playing New York, New York for him now because you know they'll think it's cool. You can tell he thinks it's cool, 'cause he's swinging his drink in time like a conductor. But now he's looking up again and saying:

"Hey! Play the Polonaise!"

What do you do now, apprentice journeyman? You just started playing 'something snappy' for him, and now he wants to impress his girlfriends by acting like he knows 'the Polonaise.' Well, O.K.; take a look at the suggestions below and see which one you'd be most comfortable with:

a) Start playing 'the Polonaise' right in the middle of New York, New York. Add a boogie bass to it. Make it rock a little. People will laugh at this.

b) Stop playing right in the middle of New York, New York. Stand up behind the keys and say apologetically: *"I'm sorry, sir; I may be a saloon pianist, but I do have honor. Horowitz is playing 'the Polonaise' with the symphony tonight, and I promised I wouldn't play it until he got done at the concert hall."*

c) Look at him like he's weird. You've practiced squinting

quizzically in the mirror for this.

d) Keep playing New York, New York and look up at him questioningly. Repeat what he just said: 'the Polonaise?' When he nods 'yes,' ask him dead seriously:

"Which one did you want?"

When you see the look of confusion on his face, try this:

"Did you want the Siberian Polonaise; that rolling E-flat minor thing, or the Polonaise-Fantaisie in A-flat?"

Before he gets a chance to shrug his shoulders, continue with:

"Did you want the F-sharp minor masterpiece by maestro Fredrique, or the slower, lugubrious-by-comparison C-sharp minor cliff-hanger?"

When it becomes obvious that he doesn't know what the hell you're talking about, you graciously let him off the hook. Smile and say:

"I know. You want the MILITARY POLONAISE!"

With vigor, you enthusiastically thunder out the opening chords to one of the most famous tunes in the world, then slowly slog back into New York, New York when you think he's heard enough. Play New York, New York with such a dearth of feeling that they can't wait for you to finish.

Well, how'd you do? Can you guess which one the journeyman did? Uh - oh. I see you caught on fast. You got me before I had a chance to trick you on this one.

Yes, dear reader, the journeyman has done all of the above, he's ashamed to admit. In the truest tradition of fighting fire with fire, one fights a smart-ars by being a worse smart-ars. The most important thing to keep in mind is that no matter what happens, you have to still be there at the end of the night to get paid. Therefore, you have to outlast the jerks who come in and do this.

So practice up, ladies and gentlemen. Get those chords and runs just right. Allegro! Vivace! Can YOU play the Polonaise yet? Faster! Schnell! Mit feeling, now! Schnell!

TOM ANDERSON

It was nearing St. Patrick's Day around Bill Bailey's Saloon in the early 80's. Tom Anderson was one of the more colorful characters who hung around the place, always dressed immaculately in a three-piece suit, watch-chain, and sometimes a dressy hat. Tom is one of the jet-blackest African-Americans I have ever known, and this usually quiet man told and acted out the following story to the whole bar one night as the Journeyman Piano Player paused between tunes:

"Hey Bob, I always get down around St. Patrick's day. Real down."

Since the piano was on a small stage behind the bar, everyone could tune into the conversation as I answered Tom, seated at the far end of the bar:

"Oh, yeah, Tom? Why's that?"

"I'm afraid to go out and be Irish anymore. I don't know how."

"Oh, come on, Tom," I answered. "You don't have to know how to be Irish. Just go out and have a good time."

"Not after what happened last time, Bob. Not after what happened last time."

Obviously, now, everyone in the place wanted to hear what he had to say. So I let him begin:

"O.K., Tom. What happened last time?"

"Well, you see," he started, "I always wanted to take my lady out on St. Patrick's Day and DO THE TOWN UP GREEN. Ya' know what I mean? I always wanted to DO THE TOWN UP GREEN."

"Yeah," I answered, "I think we all do."

"Well," he started, "a couple years ago, I decided I was going to do exactly that. I had to save everything I made for six weeks at that rotten desk job I have, so then on the night in question, I rented a kelly green tuxedo, tails n' all, green top hat to match, and picked up my walking cane. I rented a beautiful green gown for my lady, and we called for the limo."

"Sounds fabulous," injected someone.

"Yes, sir," he continued. "We told that limo driver:

'TAKE US TO WHERE IT IS THAT THEY SING AND DANCE AND DO THE IRISH JIG! 'TIS THE EMERALD ISLE WE CRAVE, ME LADDY, SO TAKE US WHERE THE RIVER SHANNON FLOWS! POSTHASTE! BEGORAH!'"

I inserted a few strains from some Erin Isle tune to enhance his story at this point. Anderson had arisen and walked to center-bar, speaking dramatically now as he 'got into character.'

"*Ah, yes, me little Irish lassie, we went directly to The Old Shillelagh Irish Pub in downtown Detroit. We alighted at curbside arm in arm, and strode within. There was mirth and rollicking from stem to stern when we entered. Even at five o'clock in the afternoon, frivolity was in full sway.*"

"*It usually is on St. Patty's Day,*" answered someone. "*They really go for it.*"

"*Ah, indeed they do!*" brogued Anderson. "*So in keeping with the spirit, I took me lady up to the bar, pulled out a ten dollar bill, tipped me hat to the bartender and said:*

"*'Give us two of those Old Bushmill's Irish Whiskeys, and keep the change, sir, PLEASE!'*

"*With that, I slapped down the tenner on the bar and we turned to view the festivities.*"

"*So far, so good,*" said the journeyman. "*So you're telling us that you had a good time?*"

Anderson recoiled:

"*Good time?*" he asked, incredulously. "*Did you say 'we were having a good time?' Well, let me tell you my friend, that we stood there watching the gala in progress, and then I turned to pick up our drinks. But do you think I found drinks?*"

Anderson was scowling, but now he continued:

"*No, sir, we certainly did NOT find drinks. Instead, I found - THE BARTENDER!*"

Anderson shifted his position to portray the bartender glowering over the bar at him. Then:

"*He hadn't moved an inch from where I'd last seen him, and he was SCOWLING THROUGH HIS RUDDY RED BEARD AT ME!*"

"*Oh, come on, Tom,*" said someone. "*Bartenders don't care if you're black or white.*"

"*Black or white?*" he yelled, the tension rising dramatically. "Did I say anything about black or white? No, sir, I said he was SCOWLING AT ME, so I repeated our order, this time with feeling:

"*'Barkeep! Me lady and me would like to have TWO OLD BUSHMILL'S IRISH WHISKEYS, AND KEEP THE CHANGE PUH-LEASE!' Then I turned to observe the gala again.*"

"*What, were they out of Old Bushmills?*" asked someone.

"*Out of Old Bushmills?*" he screamed in amazement. "I don't think 'out's' the right word. 'Out of Old Bushmills?' Well, sir, the whole place had quieted down to watch us now. Something - I said SOMETHING - was up! So I turned around once more to look at the barkeep and he was still there, leaning bodaciously on the bar. So I straightened my kelly green bowtie, looked him straight in the eye, raised my finger to let him know I meant business, and said:

"Barkeep! We'll have..."

At this point, Anderson began acting the role of the bartender as well. He would now alternate back and forth, portraying either the 'bartender' or 'Tom.'

Bartender, scowling across bar:
"YOU'LL HAVE TWO OLD BUSHMILLS IRISH WHISKEY?"
Tom, somewhat taken aback:
"Uh, yes," he answered himself, "and keep the change..."
Bartender, screaming:
"OLD BUSHMILLS? YOU WANT TWO OLD BUSHMILLS?"
Tom, becoming intimidated:
"Yes sir, and..."
Bartender, beating his fists on the bar and thundering:
"YOU'RE IN HERE WANTING TWO OLD BUSHMILLS IRISH WHISKEYS? WE DON'T SERVE THAT PROTESTANT SHIT IN THIS PLACE!"
'Tom' was now devastated as he acted on:
"But - but - we only wanted..."
"This is an IRISH bar! Not a bloody Orange Flag Special!" screamed the 'bartender,' as Tom quivered in fear.
"But - but - sir!" He was wringing his hands in emotion by now.
"But sir, we were only trying, uh..."
"YES?" demanded the 'bartender.'
"We, uh, we, uh..."
"YOU WANT OLD BUSHMILLS, DO YOU?" the barkeep stormed.
"We were only trying - TO BE COOL!" blurted Tom in desperation.
"COOL?" raved the 'bartender.' "They're hangin' men an' women for the wearin' of the green, and you're talking about Old Bushmills and 'being cool?'"
Anderson went down on his knees now as he sobbed pitifully:
"I'm sorry, sir! I'm sorry! Say whatever you want, sir, but - PLEASE DON'T HURT ME!"

If memory serves correctly, the barmaid came along at this point and gave him a glass of Old Bushmill's as he lay 'weeping' on the bar. The whole saloon exploded in applause for this performance, and the Journeyman Piano Player played a few strains from 'Her Endearing Young Charms.'

At no time did Tom imply that anything about this episode was racist, only that he'd unwittingly asked for the wrong thing in the wrong place. I can still see him weeping on the bar and pleading:
*"But sir, we were only trying ...**TO BE COOL!**"*

ONE FOR THE ROAD

The professional pianist has to be a professional driver as well. To begin with, if you don't show up at the job, then you obviously aren't going to get paid. But secondly, and more importantly, the professional pianist is on the road at the same time the drunks are let loose from the bars. Avoiding accidents becomes the primary concern underlying the entire business. It becomes, literally, survival. A few examples follow.

Alcohol is poison to me. I almost died from incidents related to alcohol addiction, so now I don't allow it into me in any shape or form. Even foods that have been cooked in wine are taboo. Although everyone is quick to point out that alcohol evaporates during the cooking process, I am even quicker to point out that it does NOT evaporate when cooked in a microwave oven. On August 15, 1974, I crawled away from my last experience with alcohol and vowed it would never happen again. I viewed the ensuing months of shaking, shivering, and DTs as a vicious animal inside me, dying hard.

My experiences with alcohol taught me how drunks think. They think they are in control. They think, like I once did, that a straight, darkened highway is safe at 130 miles per hour, simply because the car can do it. (The next night, sober and on the same stretch of road, I was afraid to go over 65). Once you realize that drunks will think this way, no amount of precaution seems to be enough.

Drunks can't remember to dim the headlights. That's the first tipoff. Drunks also, unless they are passing-out drunk, will still drive on the right side of the road. This is why, when approaching a blind curve on an expressway, I will get out of the fast lane and into the inside lane. This saved my life once when, sure enough, a drunk came around the curve going the wrong way down the expressway. Oh, yes; he was in the right-hand lane alright. He must have thought that the two lanes on his left were a little strange, and the cars swerving around to get out of his way were all idiots. I slammed on the brakes, turned to look back for an explosion (which I didn't see), and never heard any news about a wreck that night. He must have, miraculously, survived somehow.

But drunks aren't the only danger on the road. I have always figured, almost simplistically, that the more I am on the road, the more likely I am to be hit by someone. Therefore, I play the percentages. I stay away from, among other things, eighteen-wheelers.

Any set of statistics will tell you that more than half the trucks on the road will fail a brake inspection. I drove a logging truck for years, so I know how difficult and expensive it is for owners to keep up the equipment. I know that the money from the load that the truck may be carrying is already spent on many other things before any of it is left over for repairs. The drivers know how to down-shift to slow the truck, because they also know the brakes aren't going to slow it down regardless of what hapless piano player happens to be in front of it.

Tires on eighteen-wheelers are just as bad or worse. They'll rotate the worn tires to the inside position, and if you ever want to know the financial condition of the trucking company, just look at their tires. So I adopted the rule, 'tis safer to be behind 18 wheelers than in front of them.' This, however, is only marginally true. One week before this writing, a tire exploded on a truck some fifty yards in front of me. The explosion actually shook my car as the tire parts went sailing high above the expressway, and one piece of shrapnel hitting my grill like a rocket. I swerved into the median ditch to avoid the tire sections coming down at the windshield and hid behind the steering wheel as they crashed around me. When the smoke finally cleared, the Journeyman Piano Player continued on to play, tuxedo clad, in the elegant Fox Theatre in Detroit. If I, or anyone else, had been next to that tire when it blew, that person would probably be dead right now.

Another interesting aspect of survival driving emerged from the car-jacking/kidnapping/cement-block-dropping/drive-by-shooting mentality that permeates Detroit. Driving through the murder capital of the country is a veritable gamut-run. To perhaps familiarize yourself with it, take the following multiple- choice test:
1. You are driving home after a gig. It's 1:00 in the morning on the I75 expressway. You drive in the left-hand lane because:
   a) You are going faster than the other cars
   b) You want to outrun the other cars
   c) You want to position yourself so that if someone drives up pointing a pistol at you, they have to hold it right underneath their chin, assuming they're right handed.

Did you choose 'c?' Good. That's the correct answer. Any street punk knows that if they fire a pistol inside their own car, it will break their eardrums. Therefore, if you are in the left-hand lane, the punk will either have to shoot left-handed at you with his arm out the window (not a good idea; he'll likely drop the gun and miss, too) or fire the thing right-handed from underneath his chin. The punks know this might kill even them. They prefer to have an associate punk in the car with them who can get the pistol just out the passenger-side window. It's the 'punk-friendly' method. So, obviously, drive on the 'punk-unfriendly' side.

Guns are an unpleasant subject with me. I had a tire shot off my car on I75 one night in the middle of Detroit. Since there was a C.B. radio in my car, I was able to call for help, keeping in mind that thieves and hoods in Detroit all have C.B.s in their cars. When someone would ask for my location, I would tell them to identify themselves according to certain police codes. One character actually responded with a correct code, so I told him that when he came to my car, park in front-NOT IN BACK- of me. I told him I would shoot anyone who pulled up in back of me. He never did show up, but the State Police eventually arrived, I changed the tire, and continued on home. Now you are ready for the next question:

2. You are nearing a road overpass. Of course, you're in the left lane. When you approach the overpass, you:
  a) speed up
  b) stay in the left lane
  c) quickly switch lanes and change speed just before going under the bridge

Did you choose 'c' again? Good for you. It shows that you are gaining intuition in this jungle-type game. (Does it remind you of looking into treetops for leopards before going under the tree?) Yes, of course; you quickly switch lanes and change speed to throw off some imbecile who's going to drop a cinder block on you. That's right; you can't see him. You won't see him. No one who ever gets hit saw him. Remember, road overpasses are uncaged, meaning that they're not enclosed in chain-link mesh to prevent the throwing of anything bigger than tennis balls. You successfully dodge a block-dropper just once, and you win the rest of your life. Give yourself two more points and move forward to question 3.

  3. You are approaching a red light in the city. You:
   a) stop and wait for it to turn green
   b) time your car speed to hit the light just as it turns green
   c) since two-thirds of the Detroit Police force has been laid off or fired by mayor Coleman Young, you run the red light knowing that you won't get a ticket.

Aha! I've caught you! You don't know whether to choose 'b' or 'c,' do you? Confused? Don't be. That's dangerous, too. Detroit driving demands that you don't spend the time to decide which one is right; you simply do one or the other, or both. But here's your answer.

They're both correct. Both 'b' and 'c' apply to the red light situation. You time your car to keep moving, but if that's not possible you just run the light. The only other thing to add is that you didn't run the light only because the police are all laid off. You ran it because a moving target is a difficult target. If you stop, the punks will slam a car into your rear end and rob you of wallet, clothes, car, and possibly your life when you get out to protest.

The list of defensive and survival driving goes on, but you'll have to stay tuned for another installment. Whole tomes can be written about this subject.

The Sweet Violets standing on street corners looking for work
Photo by Joanne Domka, 1991

TAKE HIM AWAY...

I was playing ragtime at a popular beer hall in Detroit in the late 1980's. This colorful place was a favorite hangout for a wide variety of people, ranging from college swill-em'-down yahoos to prosecutors and federal judges. On the night in question, during a rousing sing-a-long session, I looked up from the piano long enough to notice the managers and owners hastening out the door en masse. Realizing that something was amiss, I calmly finished the tune and discreetly sauntered outside to see what was up. It didn't take long to find out. A street punk had grabbed a woman's purse as she left, dragging her down the middle of the road, kicking and screaming. The parking lot guard, built like a small gorilla, had pounced on the punk and was holding him face down in the gutter now as a small crowd gathered.

A phone call was made to the police. Fortunately, there was a police mini-station three blocks up the street. Unfortunately, however, there were no police in it, due to mayoral budget cuts. It would turn into a forty-five minute vigil awaiting the ultimate arrival of cops. During this time, certain local residents became angered over the apprehension of one of their punks:

"Hey! What you holding him for?"

"He tried to steal that woman's purse."

"Is that all he did? Well, he ain't got a job. He's just trying to feed his family. Let 'im go before we get pissed off!"

Certain customers showed up conspicuously bearing guns. I got my car out of the parking lot and parked it next to the scene in progress, thus protecting the guard and owners from drive-by gunfire. Other local residents proved to be sympathetic to the owners:

"Caught you a thief, eh? Good. Get him the hell out of here."

Eventually the police showed up, handcuffed the hood, and took him away. It was then that events started to fall into place rather nicely.

A county prosecutor happened to be a customer in the place that night. When he heard what had happened, he commented about the safety of his wife and kids who were with him. As luck would have it, that same prosecutor was assigned the very case in question in the courtroom. He used the hood's lengthy record and blatant attempted crime to have the judge deny bail, thus keeping the punk in the slammer and away from the beer hall until the trial date arrived.

Two nights later, another prominent guest showed up at the beer hall. George was an official in the Detroit probation department. When I relayed to him what had happened, he looked at me and said:

"This is my favorite beer hall, Bob. Tell me the name of this bastard, and I'll see that he doesn't get out for a while."

George ultimately reviewed the punk's record and made his recommendations to the judge. The judge imposed a minimum of three years in jail before parole could even be considered.

Just after trial time, a third noteworthy guest showed up. Kerry was an official at the county jail. His job was to assess prisoners and make recommendations as to when they should be paroled. Upon learning of the scene that took place in front of his favorite beer hall, he agreed that this hood, based on what had gone on outside and the punk's previous record, would be closely scrutinized before he'd ever be considered for parole.

There's a famous line from the New Orleans classic, Buddy Bolden's Blues:
"I thought I heard Judge Fogerty say,
Thirty days in the marketplace, take him away..."

Well, as of this writing, the dude's been in the 'marketplace' for a lot more than thirty days. There should be more of the same; more of the same.

THE PARABLE OF LETTUCES AND CABBAGES

Have you ever wondered why it is difficult to find published rags by today's composers? Good composers, such as Glenn Jenks, Jack Rummel, or Scott Kirby, to name just a few? Well, the answer lies in the difficulty involved in getting publishers to even show passing interest in what you have. Publishers already have their own business problems - (*"How's that deal going that we started in California last month? What do you mean 'only fair?' We'll lose our butts on this unless you step up production, sales, and advertising! Get moving, do you hear? GET MOVING!"*)

Well, do you get the idea? Now, with this kind of pressure going on in the back office, some guy comes in the front door with some pretty sounding music and tries to get someone's attention. After many attempts to interest various publishers in my own rags and music, I finally came up with what I call 'The Parable of Lettuces and Cabbages.' It goes as follows:

Once upon a time, a young musician walked into the house of the Agha-Publisher. He found the great man seated behind his 1920's wooden desk befouling the room with cigar smoke and wearing a ill-fitted cardigan sweater that was one-hole off-buttoned. The Agha-Pub resembled a cross between Mr. McGoo and an oracle, and had a mirthful smirk on his face. (Sometimes known as a 'smirthfulmirk'). The young musician spoke to him respectfully:

Y.M.: *"Greetings, Mr. McSmirthful. I have travelled many miles to bring you rags."*

McSmirthfulmirk: (interlocking his fingers and spinning his thumbs in a blur) *"Ohh-hh? You DON'T SAY?"*

Y.M.: *"Yes, oh Holy One. I believe they are the most beautiful rags in the world. Would you like to hear them?"*

McSM.: (in the style of McGoo): *"Ye-eESS! DO play them for me!"*

The young musician then filled the halls with beautiful music. Women from the harem strolled out onto balconies to listen as the music drew them from their chambers, and servants stopped moving momentarily to bask in heavenly strains the likes of which were never before heard in the kingdom. When he was finished, the young musician turned to the Agha-Pub, who was obviously pleased. He spoke respectfully once again:

Y.M.: *"Are you pleased, oh Divine One?"*

McSM.: *"I am pleased beyond all measure, young musician. Truly, those are the most beautiful rags in the world."*

Y.M.: *"I am honored by your words, oh great and honorable Agha-Pub. Now, sir, and with all due respect, would you like to publish them?"*

McSM.: (smiling idiotically) *"No-ooOOO!"*

Y.M.: *"But, uh, you confuse me, oh sage of the earth, wind, and water. If you think my rags are the most beautiful, why won't you publish them?"*

McSM.: *"Because, wha-Ha!, I cannot SELL them! But I have good news for you, young musician. I can sell LETTUCES AND CABBAGES for you! Bring them to me in crates, and we can do business! Your name will be on every camel caravan and bill of lading between here and Rangoon! You'll be famous! I can see the headlines now - 'R. Milne (Ragtimist), becomes R. Milne (Cabbologist)!' Servants! Bring this man a wheelbarrow and hoe! Hasten! Hasten!"*

The Agha-Pub, his mood suddenly becoming dark and serious, then turned to the young musician and said:

*"Tell me, oh one of so few years..., **what kind of fertilizer do you use?**"*

End of Agha-Parable

TALES OF THE RED GARTER

When Doug Jacobs started the Red Garter Saloon in downtown Detroit, about 1967, I was the piano player with his band. We cranked out Dixieland and sing-a-long six nights a week in a basement saloon that resembled a speakeasy. Many weird antics took place in 'the Garter' every night, mostly spontaneous, vaudeville-type insanity, such as keeping a pitcher of beer on the grand piano for the band. Whenever a band member needed a beer, they'd just thrust a mug in my direction, I'd empty the whole pitcher over their glass and outstretched hand, and the remainder of the beer cascaded to the stage floor. A waiter would quickly appear with a fresh pitcher for the next band member who ran dry.

The Red Garter Band was a select group of goof-offs. Nothing was beneath us, including a pie-in-the-face routine we pulled off once with an agreeable sit-in banjo player. He went up on the stage during one of our breaks and began strumming both furiously and horribly, creating an awful sound in the place. Soon, a waiter was manuevering his way between the tables, with pie:

"*Excuse me, folks. Excuse me, sir. I'll take care of this for you right away, sir...,*" and when he reached the stage, he pied the banjo player to the shouts and cheers of the crowd.

Insanity of this order occurred nightly and we were used to it, because we expected it. Some things, however, we were not able to anticipate and were constantly perplexed by, and many of them came from our tuba player, Darryl 'Ding' Bronson.

Ding passed away a few years ago, and I don't want to do anything to discredit his name (which I've changed, of course). However, Ding was strange. He was strange in a nice, lovable way. To begin with, he had a photographic memory, so we knew he was no dummy. We could show him a piece of music, he'd look at it once, and then play it on the bandstand without flaw. He could remember things he'd seen in great detail, long after he'd seen them.

The thing Ding wasn't good at, and I try to word this very carefully, was 'tact.' Maybe 'tact' isn't the right word, but I'll give a few examples here and maybe, with your help, we'll find the right word.

Consider, for instance, that Ding owned a Volkswagen bus. When he went to sell it, he couldn't understand why I didn't want to buy it, and he actually became angry with me:

"*Bob! How long have I known you? You're a friend of mine and you know there's nothing wrong with that bus! Why won't you buy it? Come on, Bob; I need the money!*"

The fact that I had absolutely no use for the bus and already had a perfectly reliable car meant nothing to Ding. He'd fight with me during our breaks, and then we'd all go back on the bandstand where he'd astonish the crowd with his musical ability. Next break, it would be something else.

This time I was standing with some people when Ding, conspicuous in his red-striped vest, band attire, and having been onstage for at least two hours already, walked by me. He was smiling a Stan Laurel smirk as he approached a table full of well-dressed people. The conversation went something like this:

"*Hello. I'm the tuba player with the band.*"

"*Oh, hi,*" they replied.

(Pause. Then...)

"*May I join you?*"

"*Oh, yes; please do!*" they responded, having no choice, really.

Ding sat down. He smiled to them, then turned to a man dressed in a business suit and said:

"*Would you like to buy a bus?*"

Maybe 'direct' is the word I'm looking for here, but also, maybe not. Let's search further for the correct wording:

Having no luck selling the bus, Ding resorted to another method. One night, as the band took a break, we were tired and weary from the night-after-night pounding that we had to put out. Sometime late in the evening, I wandered into the men's room. At least there was a little shelter from the noise in there, so I was in no hurry to leave. I washed my hands, combed my hair, splashed cold water on my face, was towelling off and stretching when I noticed something I hadn't seen before. A string was tied around a water pipe up in a corner at the ceiling. My eyes slowly followed the string down between the paint cracks in the wall (it was hard to see in the dim light) until I saw it end, about three feet above a urinal. Curious, I walked over to see what this was all about. There was a piece of paper tied to the end of this string, one of those pages torn loose from a spiral binding and thus having all kinds of shredded edges on it, and this sign was hanging at eye-level for anyone standing in front of the urinal. It read:

For Sale:
Bus
See Tuba Player

Maybe 'direct' isn't the right word, either. Let's see, now. Maybe this next example will help shed further light on the wording:

Ding had a few other 'strange' ideas, and one of them surfaced when Hudson's Department Store, a major institution in Detroit for decades, hired a trio from the Red Garter to play for a ladies luncheon. The trio was myself, Ding, and a banjo player.

We arrived on Hudson's 13th floor restaurant on the appointed day, and found the piano in the middle of the room, in close proximity to the ladies themselves. The clientele that day consisted mostly of what appeared to be elderly ladies, sipping their tea, delighting over crumpets, and tasting perhaps the chicken pot pie. We set up around the piano and began playing lilting tempos. No need, here, to thunder out the 'Saints' or the 'Robert E. Lee' medley (which Ding politely explained to a guest who requested it, 'we can't do that one in here, ma'am. It's one of our biggies.') We puttered along on medium-tempo tunes, and Ding played 'Oomp...oomp, Oomp...oomp' to the beats.

After about half an hour of gentle dinner music, we began playing 'Peg O' My Heart.' Ladies looked up from their luncheons and smiled their approval as we lilted along and smiled back to them. That is, until we came to the line in the song that goes:

> "Since I heard your lilting laughter
> It's your Irish heart I'm after..."

At this point I heard the 'oomping' stop as Ding leaned forward into the microphone to croon:

> "Heidy-didy, Christ Almighty,
> How I'd like to get in your nighty..."

"Oomp...oomp...'

In shock, I looked quickly around the room to see how much damage had been sustained. Ladies were sitting frozen in mid-bite, staring across their tables at each other. I hoped that they would think they'd misunderstood something, and as I realized that Ding couldn't differentiate between the barroom and the luncheon special, fear began to overtake me. What would he do next? Now, we were going into the second strain of Peg O' My Heart, and I knew that he wouldn't sing the same line over again. Since he'd done it once, he wouldn't do it again. Right? Wro-o-o-ong. Suddenly, again, the 'oomping' stopped and I could see him leaning into the microphone again. I could also see the ladies nervously stirring in their seats. Then:

"Hiedy-didy..."

This time I cut him off. I whirled around on the bench and stage-whispered:
"NO! DON'T SING THAT!"
But instead of backing off, Ding's eyes flashed at me in the same manner as when he was furious over the bus incident. Now, sitting in the middle of the ladies 13th floor luncheon special with everyone in the place watching in stone silence, Ding yelled in rage at me:
"WHY NOT? WE SING IT ALL THE TIME AT THE CLUB! COME ON, BOB, YOU KNOW WE DO!"

He was too mad at me to play the tuba for a moment, so I sat up there smiling to little old ladies, playing 'Peg O' My Heart,' and wondering how much longer I was stuck up there on this job. The fact that Ding, on our ten-minute break, stood in the lunch line, got himself a three-course lunch complete with salad and dessert, then sat down and spent a half hour eating it while the banjo player and myself played the rest of the job was rather welcome. I think the ladies appreciated it, also.

These kinds of aberrations, once known, can become part of a working musician's bag of credentials. You want to highlight various artists on their strong points, and steer them away from their weak points. Therefore, we steered Ding away from sensitive social gatherings. Another contributing factor in that decision was the time when an elderly piano player had passed away, the band attended the funeral, and then proceeded to the widow's house for the wake. She greeted us at the door where Ding, spying the dinner spread in the adjoining room, remarked excitedly:
"Oh, boy! Free eats!"

When Ding had it in his mind that something was supposed to happen, nothing could change his mind. I remember waking up early one morning, hearing the sound of a motor in my driveway. I recognized it as the sound of Ding's bus, and I knew before I even got out of bed what had happened. We had a recording session the next day, and Ding had driven thirty miles and stopped by to pick me up a day early. It was a nice gesture, and we all get mixed up on dates from time to time, but what was noteworthy in this instance was his reaction when I informed him of the mistake:

"*Tomorrow?!*" he said, incredulously. "*So that's why the babysitter didn't show up!*"

I asked him what he'd done. He surely didn't leave his little child alone at home.

"*No, of course not,*" he replied. "*I drove down the block and dragged the babysitter from her house. I told her that if she was going to be my babysitter, she'd better start showing up on time. Now I have to take her home again.*"

Are you finding any words to help me with? It's probably becoming clear that no one word is going to suffice. But let's have one more example now in our quest for the truth. Consider this one, folks:

Doug Jacobs, the band leader, took the band out on some job that went on for days. The job involved the use of a double-decker bus, moving around to many locations, transporting customers, and taking a band along throughout the entire week. Finally, when it was over, Doug asked Ding to deposit the funds he'd been paid at the bank. This was not at all unusual, as Ding was well-known and totally trustworthy, so Doug gave Ding an envelope with about ten thousand dollars in it and sent him on his way...

It should probably be explained here that Ding could be relied upon because contrary behavior didn't occur to him. He was totally honest, and assumed that everyone else was, also. I recall, one night on the bandstand, when a shady lady of the evening came in and sat by herself at a table, eyeing the men in the place. Ding put down his tuba for a moment, leaned over to me and said, excitedly:

"*Hey, Bob! Look at that babe over there!*"

The others and I tried to explain to him that she screwed for money and was here looking for customers, but Ding couldn't believe it. She was nice looking, and that's all that mattered. On our next break he went and sat down with her, smiling his little Stan Laurel smile, and introduced himself accordingly:

"Hello. My name's Ding. I'm the tuba player with the band. May I join you?"

As she squirmed in her seat from this business interruption, Ding was smiling and opening a little package of cookies he'd brought with him that night...

With this in mind, you may be able to understand the nature of what happened next. I was sitting at home, about 6:00 one evening, when the phone rang. It was Doug Jacobs, and he was frantic. Frantic isn't the right word, either. Maybe 'hysterical.' Perhaps every word in the psychosis primer would be suitable. Anyways, when I picked up the phone, this is what I heard:

"Bob! I'm ruined! I'm screwed! Everything I've ever worked for is out the fucking window!"

"What?" I tried to reason, adding, "Control yourself, Dougie. Calm down! What's wrong?"

"Ding!" he screamed. "That idiot! I can't believe it! Why me? Why me?"

"Doug," I tried to reason again, "what's going on? Tell me, my friend; tell me."

Doug was virtually shrieking into the phone, and it went something like this:

"That idiot! He called me two minutes ago and said, 'Hey, Doug, this is Ding. I only got enough money for one minute on the phone, but the bank was closed so I left the money with Joe at Annie's Donut Shop on Michigan Avenue. He's sitting at the counter waiting for you, so...'

"AND THEN THE PHONE WENT DEAD WHEN HE RAN OUT OF MONEY!!!"

I, of course, could think of nothing to say. I could hear Doug Jacobs screaming on the other end of the phone, so the next time he stopped to take a breath, I told him:

"Doug, for Pete's sake, GET DOWN THERE! STOP TALKING TO ME, HANG UP THE PHONE, AND GET MOVING!"

"Why?!" he screamed. "The money's gone, for Christ's sake! What's the point now?"

It was clear that Doug couldn't think straight, so I urged him to get off his duff and get moving. He finally did.

There was, however, a happy ending to this. Someone actually put the money - all ten thousand dollars of it - into an envelope and put it behind the counter to await Doug Jacobs. He informed me that he was so weak, after finding it safely awaiting him, that he collapsed at the counter and sucked up coffee for half an hour. Ding brushed off the incident, saying:

"Oh? What was wrong with that? I go in there all the time and I know those people."

We all loved Ding Bronson, and none of us want to discredit him in any way. He was a great musician, and also a great character.

And he certainly kept us on our toes, no question.

TIME OFF

A prominent attorney is a member of a Dixieland band which includes the Journeyman Piano Player. One summer's day, in the early 1990's, we were booked to play an ice-cream social at a rural location, starting at two o'clock in the afternoon. I called Al, the attorney, to make sure he could play the gig with us:

"Hi, Al. Can you play that ice-cream social next week?"

"Sure can. I've got a murder trial I have to be at, but I think it'll be over by then."

"What?" blurted the amazed journeyman. "What if it isn't over?"

"Don't worry about it," he answered. "I'll be there."

Mildly concerned, I put it aside until the night before the gig when I called Al back to confirm his presence:

"Hi, Al. Is the trial over yet?"

"No."

"Oh, God! What'll we do?"

"Don't worry about it, Bob. It'll be over by noon. I'll shoot right out there."

Needless to say, we all had a certain amount of apprehension over his arrival. The band arrived at the ice-cream social the next day, and we all looked out from under a large tent wondering whether of not we would see Al's car pulling into the parking lot. As two o'clock neared, we decided we'd probably have to start without him. But then, here came his car, up the road and into the parking lot. Al arrived on stage in full regalia; a wide-striped shirt and gold embossed vest to go with the Dixieland act.

"I see your murder trial is over," said I.

"No, it isn't," he replied as he sat down and readied himself to play.

Noting that this was Friday afternoon and the lawyer was on the bandstand rather than in the courtroom, I cautiously asked:

"Well, if the trial's not over, whose defending the client?"

"No one," he answered, and then nonchalantly let loose with this classic:

"I told the judge: 'uh, look, judge, I've got a gig.'"

"What?!" I blurted. "You told the judge... What'd he say?"

"Well," answered Al, "he said, 'if you've got a gig, let's put him back in the slammer. We'll continue this later.'"

I was dumbstruck. Finally:

"They put him back in jail until next Monday?"

It got worse:

"No," he answered. *"I'm tied up until the middle of next month. We'll pick up in August where we left off today."*

I couldn't believe what I was hearing. Finally:

"What about this client? He just has to sit in the can until then?"

Al looked up at me and said:

"Bob, he blew a guy's head off with a 357. Five guys saw him do it. He'd lost a checkers game for twenty dollars, pulled out a pistol and blew this guy's head to pieces. I'm supposed to try to get him off on a technicality, which is about as appealing as going swimming in a septic tank. Fuck him. Let's play some ragtime."

The Journeyman Piano Player began playing this particular gig with a decided sense of awe. It took me a while to get into the swing of things after hearing that story, but there was one thing in particular I did notice: I noticed how much this same lawyer seemed to become part of the music itself. He was lost in it. He moved to it. He smiled at its little highs and lows as he escaped from the horrors of his real life for a while. He totally immersed himself in his instrument and the moving rhythms he was helping to create.

For now, the jungle was a totally different world as he closed his eyes, played his horn, and went with the flow. Today, the music was for him.

OF CHAOS, MIRTH, AND SORROW

The piano business in Detroit took a nose dive beginning about 1983. Restaurants were closing, hotels were being foreclosed upon, and all the usual business declines were being felt in city that couldn't control crime. Bizarre events that depicted lawlessness and chaos were taking place. One such story, which was related across the country via national media, happened a block away from Bill Bailey's Bar, which I owned at the time.

At five o'clock on a summer's afternoon, a woman pulled into the drive-through lane of a Kentucky Fried Chicken establishment. With two cars ahead of her, she was waiting in line when a gang of thugs walked up and began pounding on the roof of her car. Seemingly unafraid, she rolled down the window and looked out at them. One demanded her purse and money, but instead she raised a pistol and blasted him at point-blank range. The thug thrashed across the grass for a few moments before the other hoods put him in a car and sped away. The lady continued to wait in line.

When she reached the drive-through window, her first words were:
"How much is that two-piece chicken dinner you have?"
The attendant told her the price, to which she replied:
"O.K. Give me one of them, an order of fries, and a Coke."
The attendant prepared the order, she paid for it, and after he had returned her change she turned and looked back toward the grass.
"Did I hit that guy?" she asked.
"Most definitely," the attendant replied.
"Then I'm goin' home where I got a bigger gun," she answered before driving off.

This information became known after the local hospital had the gunshot victim, dead by now, brought in by the other hoods. The hospital called the police, the police ended up at the Kentucky Fried establishment, and we later heard the story from the same police that hung out in Bill Bailey's Bar.

Another story that made the rounds happened in a place I was playing in the night it happened, about one year after the previous incident. The parking lot guard in southwest Detroit was knifed by an assailant and stuffed into his guard shack. (He lived, somehow.) The assailant then donned the guard hat and jacket and began escorting customers to their cars as they left the place. Of course, they were robbed at knife-point and one woman was raped in her car. The maniac continued this act for five or ten minutes, or until he knew the police were on the way, then disappeared.

When the place closed, due to the obvious lack of business following that episode, the Journeyman Piano Player was out of another job and had to search farther than Detroit to find one. He was in luck. A festival marketplace had opened in Toledo, sixty miles south of Detroit and just across the Ohio line. A restaurant was going to have ragtime seven nights a week, and all day Saturday and Sunday. They hired myself and my wife Linda, also a professional ragtime player. The only problem was that we live sixty miles NORTH of Detroit. The job meant a 120 mile one-way drive. We accepted, and thus began 3-1/2 years of commuting long distance.

The Real Seafood Company, in the Portside Festival Marketplace, was located on the Maumee River, a major port for Great Lakes shipping traffic. Lake freighters, ocean boats from every part of the world, tourist excursion and paddlewheel boats all went up and down the Maumee, only a few scant yards from where I sat at my old Aeolian player piano entertaining guests. I took the front off so the customers could see the electric player mechanism when it was on, and have a little fun as well.

I used to put on a roll, perhaps 'Ida, Sweet as Apple Cider,' let the Aeolian play it for a moment and then stop in mid-roll. I would continue playing 'Ida' by myself. When a customer would walk up and start talking to me, I would look up and discuss whatever it was he was saying, then (when I came to the refrain where the piano roll began) I'd bump the 'Start' switch with my knee and the piano roll would begin playing. I would continue moving my hands as if still playing, but the customer would now see keys going down that I wasn't hitting. He could see the roll going around and all the little bellows opening and closing in the process. I'd then switch the piano off at the end of the phrase and play the tune to the end myself. People got a kick out of it and thought it was neat. Also, some people didn't realize I was ever really playing at all. I heard the following comment more than once as I played:

"Look, honey; they have an old player piano here."
"Yeah, I see. What's that guy doing?"
"He's pumping the pedals. These things need someone to do that."
"Oh. Well, do they have a table for us yet? I'm hungry."

My favorite reaction, however, was when some droll character simply stopped talking and watched when the player piano took over and I faked playing it. He never even cracked a smile. He watched the mechanism silently churning away as 'Ida' sailed all through the restaurant, and didn't say a word when I switched it off and continued playing myself, the piano roll no longer turning in plain sight. Finished now, I sat there with a silly smirk on my face, not knowing what to expect. He apparently didn't know what to expect either, for he just turned and walked off without saying a word. I watched him eating dinner at his table over the next hour or so, but he never even looked back at me again. Finally, I noticed he had left, and I never saw him again.

Some of the freighters going up and down the Maumee provided interesting, and sometimes hair-raising, sights. I once looked up to see an ocean freighter from overseas crawling upstream at an extremely slow speed. A quick glance explained why; the communications mast was coming dangerously close to the Anthony Wayne suspension bridge ahead. To make sure they had enough clearance, some seaman had climbed up to the top of the mast (protruding upwards about 40 feet from the command deck) and was giving hand signals to those below as to whether to proceed or not. This man then guided the ship FROM THE TOP OF THE MAST under the highest section of the Anthony Wayne Bridge as the entire restaurant sat frozen in stunned silence. We watched this man's head missing the underside of the bridge BY INCHES as the huge ship proceeded at a snail's pace underneath. And when the boat, mast, and seaman cleared the final girder, a tremendous ovation burst loose from our clientele for a feat unrivaled by any circus high-wire act I'd ever seen or heard of.

The paddlewheel boat 'Arawanna Princess' ran excursion tours either up and down the Maumee or out to the islands on Lake Erie, just a few miles downstream. 'Arawanna' was the name of a mythical Indian Princess who lived along the banks of the Maumee in the 1800's ('Maumee' was a mispronunciation of 'Miami' by early French settlers), and the paddlewheel boat now became a source of jobs for musicians. I even wrote and recorded 'The Arawanna Rag' with Kerry Price and the Rivertown Syncopators (the Sweet Violets under a different name). Ray Heitger's famous 'Cakewalkin' Jass Band' was featured regularly on the boat, as were my own Sweet Violets. Solo piano jobs came up as well, and the journeyman now picked up a job playing lunch excursions on the Arawanna.

We'd go sailing out onto the river with lunch guests. I'd play ragtime on an old spinet against the starboard rail, and captain Daryll (a good man with a good sense of humor) would narrate points of interest to the guests, generating a little intrigue (mostly hogwash) as well:

"And on the starboard side, ladies and gentlemen, is the old rumrunner's house left over from prohibition days. Some say that their ghosts can still be seen making moonshine in there, but nobody knows for sure. Look closely, folks."

Some parts of the riverfront were undergoing urban renewal and were thus no more than construction sites, while other areas and buildings, left-overs from previous decades, were just sitting empty awaiting a decision from the city fathers. One such building occupied a square block and was about five stories high. Captain Daryll and I worked up a little routine to amuse the customers with this building. As we'd float by it, he'd pick up the microphone and announce:

"And on your right, ladies and gentlemen, is the old Toledo Pianoworks Factory. It was closed and went out of business shortly after Mr. Milne began his professional playing career."

The guests would all look at me, sitting behind the piano with a pitiful grimace on my face, and mutter *"Awww,"* and other expressions of good-natured condolence, and we'd go on to the next item of interest.

One day, and whatever gods are responsible for this I'll never know, we came floating down the river again doing our usual spiel. When we drew near the old factory, Captain Daryll began his predictable lines:

"And on your right, ladies and gentlemen, is the old Toledo Pianoworks Factory. It was closed and went out of business shortly after Mr. Milne began his professional playing career."

But this time, as the guests stood looking at it, a mighty roar suddenly let loose, the building gave an ominous shudder, and then it came crashing down in a pile of bricks, dust, and debris. Daryll and I both realized at the same time what had happened; the urban renewal squad had dynamited it at the very instant we were going by with our tour, and now our guests watched the 'Toledo Pianoworks' come thundering down in a pile of trash.

I didn't know how to react, and just sat behind the piano apparently looking confused. But some woman who had watched this debacle with a deadpan expression now turned to me and said:

"You must be simply terrible."
She then turned and walked off.

The 120-mile trip home at night was a bear and, of course, it led to more exposure to dangerous situations. One night, as I drove north on a darkened, rural section of I75, I was reliving some of the amusing things we'd done that night to make long jobs more tolerable. I may have been thinking about the 'Toledo Pianoworks Factory,' or maybe about the time I turned on the player piano, pretended I was a mannequin, and sat moving my hands in slow, robotic fashion across the keys as the piano thundered out 'The William Tell Overture.' At any rate, I perked up when I noticed traffic slowing down ahead. It looked like someone had car trouble, or something. Couldn't tell yet.

I slowed down where traffic ahead of me was pulling around something in the road, and I noticed headlights off to my left. Strangely, something didn't look right about them. Still thinking about the robotics, or whatever, I pulled to the side and got out to see if someone needed help. I realized then that the lights were coming from an eighteen-wheeler lying on its side in a field. Now I could see the trailer lights behind it as well, also on its side.

"The driver might be hurt," was my first thought, so I ran between cars to cross the expressway. My next thought was so naive and

innocent that it baffles me to this day:

"What's this woman doing sleeping in the middle of the road," I wondered, as the headlights from cars to the side cast an eerie glow across her.

A girl, about eighteen years old, lay curled up on the centerline, her hands tucked under her head and an extremely peaceful expression on her face. She didn't appear to be hurt in any way, and if she were indeed injured there should be some sign of bleeding, which there wasn't. And now, about fifty yards north and square in the middle of the southbound lanes, I saw a silhouette of what looked like a tank that had been hit by a bomb. Not wanting to leave the girl 'sleeping in the middle of the road,' my eyes now adjusted to the dark until I saw another one. Yes, a second girl was 'sleeping' between me and the exploded tank, and the form of someone crawling out of the silhouetted wreckage began to form.

A couple of southbound 18-wheelers had now stopped on the other side of the 'tank,' and their lights revealed pieces of metal all over the road for at least fifty yards in each direction. The generator from a car engine lay at my feet, in fact. I reached down to touch it, and it was warm. Now, as the truck drivers jumped from their cabs and ran towards me, I could hear screams coming from the 18-wheeler on its side, and the sickening realization that these two girls weren't 'sleeping' in the road began to overtake me. I started to understand that the absence of blood on the pavement meant that her system wasn't capable of bleeding when she came sailing out of somewhere and landed there.

Police cars were on the scene within minutes, and I eventually learned that a northbound car had slammed into the 18-wheeler head-on, the girls were catapulted THROUGH THE STEEL ROOF OF THE CAR, and two young men in the car had survived somehow, with the exception of their brains. They would both be unable to think for themselves for the rest of their lives. Walking closer to the exploded tank, I then saw the holes the girls had made through the roof of a car that had been knocked inside-out. These looked similar to bullet holes through a tin can, jagged edges following the path of the projectile. By now, police were everywhere and I was in the way.

Severely shaken, I finally left to continue on home, knowing that some house along my northern route was going to be getting a phone call soon. I have two daughters, both in high school at the time, and now I imagined in horror to myself as I looked at the rows of lights along the way, that the phone was ringing at one o'clock in the morning. (Look - a light just came on in that house, and someone's father is getting up to answer it.)

"Hello?"

"Hello, sir. Are you Jane's father?"

"Yes. Is something wrong?"

"I'm afraid I have bad news for you, sir..."

The next night - in fact, the next many nights stretching into months - were different at the Real Seafood Company. I wanted to play the piano and have fun, but the horror of the images dominated my thoughts. A doctor would later tell me this is common to people who don't witness such things routinely, and that I was undergoing a normal, albeit unpleasant, shock reaction. However, I still had to sit at the piano, put life into the 12th Street Rag, play the blues when someone wanted to hear it, and laugh at the mildly funny jokes that customers tell pianists regularly. All the time, the sight of the 'bullet holes,' jagged metal, and two lifeless little bodies on a darkened highway kept popping into my mind, and everything anyone said (as well as everything I could think of to play) took on a different, twisted meaning:

"Hey, Bob! Play 'Pretty Baby.' I love that tune."

Or:

"Hey, Bob! My daughter's getting married this weekend. Better play 'Daddy's Little Girl' for me so I can cry now and get it over with."

Keep playing, Bob. Keep laughing, Bob. It makes them feel good, and maybe it'll do the same for you, if you can stand it long enough.

THE ST. JAMES INFIRMARY BLUES

It was Sunday afternoon. The Sweet Violets Ragtime Band was playing its regular gig at Nancy Whiskey's, an inner-city establishment of finer dining to which the customers brought their own food. Suffice it to say that when a customer forgot to close the screen door behind him, someone yelled:

"Close the door! You're letting the flies out!"

The Sweet Violets are a group of unflappable characters, all good musicians who get along well with each other. Of course, each one has his own characteristics. Walt Gower, the clarinet player, is always coming up with some off-the-wall joke that defies explanation, while Ted Harley, the string bass player, can stand and watch literally any chaotic scene with casual indifference. Nothing seems to bother him. Nate Panicacci, the trumpet player, will juggle his trumpet and mouthpiece in the air when he doesn't have anything else to do. John Anderson, the trombone player, is known affectionately as 'Father John' because he's always blessing everyone, while the banjo player doesn't want his name in print because he's a public figure.

On the day in question, a national scandal was taking place. A well known actor had been caught, uh, relieving himself of sexual tension inside a porno movie house. When the cops caught him, he made the unbelievable blunder of telling them his stage name, resulting in the afore-mentioned scandal. The ensuing barrage of male-related sexual jokes was relentless, and the band was now trying to conduct business in a respectable fashion as jokesters and pundits alike had a field day with this previously virgin topic. To protect the identity of the poor slob we're talking about, if indeed that's still possible, we'll simply call him 'Sweet Pea.'

The band liked to play The St. James Infirmary Blues. We liked to make up our own verses, sometimes pertinent to one of the band members. For instance, for Gower we'd sing:

> *The clarinet was playin' some blue notes,*
> *The bluest notes in town,*
> *His baby done croaked and left him,*
> *And he was feelin' down...*

At one point, we looked out the door to see a car careening out of control. The State Police had just chased some hood down the street and were now leaping out of their cars to apprehend him. After slamming his head down on the hood of the stolen car, they handcuffed him and read him his rights. The band strolled out on the steps of the saloon in mid-tune to play a few strains as the cops took him away, leaving the stolen vehicle for the wrecker. It's nice to have proper atmosphere to play in, but now we were back inside to continue our act:

> *The trumpet man was playin' some downers*
> *The band hit a mournful chord, (struhmm...)*
> *As they wheeled ma' baby down the sidewalk*
> *Feet first, and stiff as a board;*

A huge gang of people had begun to filter in. The baseball game had just let out, not far away, and some tour bus was parked close to us. Hearing the music, people returning to the bus and already half-drunk, started wandering in. Not really Dixieland fans, they didn't immediately relate to what we were playing. They were, of course, tuned into the Sweet Pea national scandal. Consequently:

"Hey! Do you guys know any tunes about Sweet Pea? Wha-haa! Wha-haa!"

Attempting to ignore them, we played on:

> *Ted Harley was eating stromboli,*
> *His bass was standing by the door*
> *Cryin' its sad, lonely heart out*
> *'Cause ma' baby, she wasn't no more;*

By now, the drunks were all over the place. The were standing inside and outside the saloon, swilling from beer and whiskey bottles. They were shouting 'Sweet Pea' jokes and making appropriate gestures to enhance their stories. Feeling a need to 'fight fire with fire,' and also not wishing to appear as nerds, the band held a brief pow-wow to see if we could come up with anything in keeping with the festivities. We ventured the following verse:

> *Oh, Sweet Pea works at Colonel Sanders,'*
> *But Lord, he's all wrung out of breath,*
> *He's workin' eighty hours in the kitchen*
> *Just choking the chicken to death;*

The place went wild. We'd never sung anything like it in our careers. We'd all heard about bands that do this kind of thing commonly, and now we found that the old adage 'if ya can't beat 'em, join 'em' actually applied to us. We quickly tried to think of another verse, and after a few instrumental choruses:

> *Now, Sweet Pea went to see Jack the Ripper,*
> *But Lord, they didn't treat him right,*
> *They said -*
> *"On Monday, Wednesday, Friday, Jack is ON, sir,*
> *But Sweet Pea - JACK'S OFF tonight!*

The bus had started its diesel engine and came down the street to load the drunks out of the bar. It tried to turn the narrow corner outside our door, but became wedged between parked cars on both sides of the street, a fire hydrant behind it, and a huge pile of rubbish outside the saloon door that must have been deposited by a dumpster with the Asian flu. Consequently, the next many minutes were taken up watching the driver (himself appearing half-smashed) inch the bus back and forth as he attempted to extricate the thing. Putrid fumes welled out of its engine compartment and through the 'yer lettin' the flies out' screen door as the band tried frantically to come up with another verse. Forget the idea of taking a break. There was nowhere to go but into the drunken mob in front of us. We felt safer staying on the stage. Finally, a brainstorm:

> *So now Sweet Pea's at the Salvation Army*
> *Oh, what's a good man to do?*
> *He says he'll give a helping hand to his brother*
> *If only they'll give him one, too...*

The bus was now crashing back and forth outside between a junk car and the trash heap as the driver became tired of screwing around. When it finally rolled over the garbage pile to bust loose, a wild cheer went up from the drunks. They hoisted their beers over their heads to salute the sot, and now turned to wave goodbye to the band. They had their predictable supply of Sweet Pea hand-signals to flip us (in good fun, of course) and were now herding for the door. But the band had come up with one more verse we wanted to lay on them. With straight face, we delivered it:

> *So, Sweet Pea's at the movies reading Playboy*
> *And the police, they can't take him away,*
> *'Cause the pages are SO STUCK TOGETHER*
> *That NOBODY KNOWS WHAT THEY SAY!*

They loved it. They exploded in applause, and then the madhouse emptied out. We could hear them screaming out the windows as they rolled off down the street. The fumes subsided somewhat and the band was finally able to take a break. We crashed down around a table, pushed the garbage to the floor and wiped spilled beer from the chairs. Once situated, Harley looked up and said:

"Hey, Bob. When's our next gig?"

The Journeyman Piano Player pulled out his note cards and squinted at them. Then:

"Tomorrow night, guys. The yacht club; tuxedos. It's the debutante's ball. The governor will be there, two state senators, and the television stations. We gotta look spiffy."

Harley looked out the door. When we saw his gaze become fixated on something, the rest of us looked out, too. It was the trash heap. Huge double tire tracks went through its steaming middle, and tin cans and crud were seeming to pop up from the compression as we watched. Harley looked back at me:

"Tuxedos? Cool!" he said. Then Gower chimed in:

"Hey, Bob. I got a good joke. Did you hear the one about..." He told the joke, but I didn't hear it. It just didn't matter any more. Like someone had once said in an impassioned barroom speech:

"It just doesn't matter; it just doesn't matter..."

It's true.

Sweet Violets at Nancy Whiskey's
Eric Mannering, trumpet, Howie Schuldt, washboard & Frank Harrison, tuba

'Twa-aaANG...'

The concert hall was almost filled as the ushers were seating the last people to be coming in. I was sitting in the wings backstage waiting to go on as my congenial host said pleasant little nothings designed to put me at ease. What he didn't realize, of course, was that I was already completely at ease, wondering what made him think I wasn't.

I was giving a lecture/concert through the Michigan Library Association, and they had sent me to a city in central Michigan, where a very elaborate library worked in conjunction with a concert hall. The nine-foot Steinway grand was a gorgeous piano, and my nervous host had even asked me to try it out prior to the concert. I did, and it played beautifully. The touch was firm but even, the tone was exquisitely balanced, and the tuning had been done by a high-quality professional who didn't have to rely on one of those electronic scopes to tell him what he was doing. The piano was magnificent.

The host finally went out on stage and delivered his opening lines to the audience, and then I went out to start the presentation. Ordinarily, at general information concerts such as this, I present the rags that people are familiar with and explain a brief history of them. They don't know the stories behind the famous rags such as Tiger and 12th Street, (commonplace to fervent ragtimers), so I try to stick to pieces that will broaden the audience's existing knowledge and give them a few new rags as well. I opened with the Maple Leaf Rag.

Following this, I went to the front of the stage and explained the circumstances under which it was written: the Maple Leaf Club in Sedalia, Missouri, Joplin's involvement with the publisher John Stark, and of course the meaning of the word ragtime, derived from 'ragged-time,' meaning syncopation. (Serious scholars refer to even more possible origins, but my rather sedate library lectures are not to be confused with the spontaneous and often comical audience eruptions/interruptions found around ragtime conventions attended by purists of the art. I recently observed a speaker interrupted by shouts of 'Rubbish! Your information is rubbish!' by a purist who disagreed with the speaker.) At any rate, following this brief introduction, I introduced Scott Joplin's beautiful Mexican serenade entitled 'Solace,' and returned to the piano to play it.

Solace is hard to describe. It reminds me of a tapestry that hangs in the air and moves with the air currents. It is subtle, beautiful, and soft, so I was trying to ease through it utilizing the softest tones I could produce from the piano. The audience was very receptive to what I was doing, and therefore when a sudden *'Twa-aaANG'* came from the mid-bass area of the piano, everyone heard it.

"What was that?!" I wondered in sudden alarm, knowing that I hadn't missed any note so bad as to produce a sound like that. I assumed that I must be imagining things and continued caressing the keys softly, but then it happened again - *'Twa-aaANG!'*

This time I knew I'd heard it, and also knew where it had come from. The 'E' below middle 'C' was playing a discord, for Pete's sake! How could this be happening? I had tried out the piano before the concert, checking every note on the keyboard, so why hadn't it done it before and why hadn't I heard it then? And here was another 'E' coming up in the bass; I pushed it down so the hammer would barely touch the strings. You guessed it: *'Twa-aaANG!'*

In the years of playing pianos, I have had to do all kinds of repair work to some of these things. I have completely removed hammer racks ON THE JOB to repair some little pin that was hanging up the action in order to complete the job and get paid. I have jerry-rigged pedal assemblies together, sometimes simply grey-taping them in place long enough to make it through to the end of the night, and I have shoved popsicle sticks down between the keys at times to keep them from wobbling sideways and hanging up on each other. But this was a new one; how in the world could a nine-foot concert grand piano be misplaying a note so badly when, only forty-five minutes prior, it had performed beautifully?

So I tried to think of what I might be doing that was different. What could there be? Another 'E' was coming up in the bass, and I was either going to have to start playing them an octave lower, transposing them to another chord-note, or figure out what the hell was causing this. Notes are notes and keys are keys and - Aha! The pedal! To make the tones even softer, I had my foot on the soft pedal, thus moving the hammers slightly to the right inside the action! (Grand pianos, to create the soft effect, shift their hammers from hitting three strings to two.) This hammer was obviously moving too far and was hitting both 'E' and the neighboring 'F' strings when it shifted position!

I took my foot off the pedal, gingerly struck the 'E,' and lo!, the thing actually worked right. Greatly relieved, as I'm sure the audience was as well, the rest of 'Solace' came off without incident. I kept my fingers on the keys and my feet off the soft pedal for the remainder of the concert.

This concert proved to be informative to me as well as to the audience, for another lesson was drilled into the journeyman. Actually, it's a lesson that came from baseball great Yogi Berra, following a horrendous loss suffered by his team in the last inning of the game. Referring to games where everyone thought they were ahead right up until the last horrifying minute when the whole thing comes falling apart at the seams, Yogi looked whimsically out over Yankee Stadium and made the classic remark, *"It ain't over till it's over."*

Truer words were never spoken. Even for journeymen piano players.

RAGTIME RICK'S

Rick and Betsy Graffing own a bar in Toledo known as Ragtime Rick's, and it lives up to its name. Rick is a fine piano player and Betsy is no slouch with a banjo. An old upright piano gets its brains beat out literally every night of the week, and the stories of barroom revelry in this barrel-house out on Reynolds Road are mind-boggling. A conspicuous sign on the side of the building gives even the uninitiated some idea of what to expect within:

Ragtime Rick's
Home of the Undefeated Barflies

The journeyman has played at Ragtime's on many different occasions. There are many pictures of celebrities who have played there hanging on the walls. Butch Thompson spent an evening playing at Rick's, Max Morath has been there, and Ray Heitger and his famous Cakewalkin' Jass Band is found quite regularly at the Wednesday night jam sessions. And these are just a few of the many touring names who stop in at Rick's on any given evening.

Rick's piano has to be seen to be believed. It is used as a ragtime piano in the truest tradition, that is, a piano that has to be equal to the physical amperage delivered to it nightly or go out in the next day's trash. The piano at Ragtime Rick's is the only piano I'm presently aware of that has a permanent repair kit attached to it.

Now, when I say 'repair kit' you're probably thinking that it has either a tuning fork or touch-up finish polish to rub into scratches, and that these are neatly stored in the piano bench. Wrong. To begin with, there is no piano bench. It's a stool that's wound together with so much grey tape, baling wire, and epoxy cement that it's sometimes hard to remember it's a piano stool.

And the piano. Oh, yes - (or should I say 'Oh, dear?'). To begin with, the open-fronted old upright has spools of piano wire sitting on top of it to replace the strings that couldn't take it that night. Wire of all descriptions sit either half-unwound (and waving in the air as the piano roars) or roll back and forth across the top of the piano as the night thunders on. Wrenches, pliers, rolls of black and grey tape, nuts, bolts, pins and screws all clatter around on this thing when Rick brings music to Toledo and the Undefeated Barflies. (Aha! You didn't think I forgot THEM, did you?)

First, let me back up and familiarize you with just who the 'Undefeated Barflies' are. They are a bunch of characters who hang out at Rick's, and include Rick (henceforth known as 'Ragtime') himself. Well, Ragtime has about thirty-five different kinds of beer on tap in this place, and these guys feel compelled to make sure that it is always fit to be served to regular customers. Therefore, they convene damn near daily to check the various beers for defects and discuss the problems of the world. One such day (it was a Thursday), they decided that the world didn't have enough softball teams. They called up another bar and the challenge was on, so they immediately formed Ragtime Rick's Barflies and threw down the gauntlet.

They needed uniforms, so they called another barfly who, since it wasn't five o'clock yet, was still at his job at a uniform company. His reply was predictable:

"What? Uniforms for you guys by Sunday?"

Impressed by their sincerity, he informed them that the only thing on hand was some crates of orange Tee shirts and caps. The Barflies were ecstatic. Now they had uniforms.

The first game of the tournament had its problems. Nobody, including the umpires, knew whether it was legal or not to call 'time out' so a baserunner could come to the dugout and have a beer. The games were having many stops and starts as the hubbub raged over this fine point until finally - and this was WRITTEN INTO SOFTBALL RULES FOR THIS LEAGUE - it was agreed that a keg of beer would be situated near third base. Anyone reaching third base could pause and down one. The Barflies, reluctant at first because of the distance involved in reaching third base, finally agreed that this would be acceptable.

Somehow or other, the Barflies won their first two games. Hence, the 'Undefeated Barflies.' It is difficult, however, to obtain information from them about any further games, and they've been playing now for six or seven years against such teams as the Toledo Hilton, the Bombay Bicycle Club, and St. Patrick's of the Heatherdowns Catholic Church.

(St. Patrick's, you question? On the same field with the Barflies? Well, dear reader, Ragtime Rick informs me that St. Patrick's is very understanding of other species of life on this planet and is thus not offended by any of the antics, shortcomings, or anamolies of the Barflies. Rick was mumbling something about 'let he who is without sin cast the first pitch,' or something like that when he tried to explain this to me. Read on.)

Some interesting videos exist of these games. In one, someone has blasted the softball between the outfielders and is running like mad around the bases. The throw that comes into home plate isn't even close to cutting him off from a home run, but now we see through the camera that the baserunner is standing out on third base having a beer and sharing it with the third baseman. Even more footage reveals a batter slugging the ball past the shortstop, then running directly to third. He was having a cool one and chatting with the third base coach when they called him 'out.'

As I researched this article, certain pieces of information had to be confirmed. For instance, when I found the heading in the rule book that read 'Bribe Rule,' (that's right; there's a heading printed in the rules entitled BRIBE RULE,) I asked Ragtime to explain this to me. He was quite nonchalant with his answer:

"Oh. The bribe rule? Well, yeah. You see, each team is allowed two bucks per game for bribes."

"Bribes?" I repeated, still not sure that I could believe this, but I was learning that to play in the Barfly league, you have to play by their rules.

"Yes," he went on. *"For instance, if you get called 'out' on strikes, the coach can come out of the dugout, hand the umpire a buck, the ump'll change the call to 'ball four,' and now you're off to first base on a 'walk.' You still have one dollar left for a later bribe."*

Ragtime must have noticed my puzzled expression, for he was then quick to add:

"But if the other team wants the call worse than you do, their coach can give the ump TWO bucks to change it back again. Now the ump yells 'YER OUT!' and you go back to the dugout. But you have a hammer 'cause the other team doesn't have any money left for bribes, and you've still got one dollar. You wait until you can inflict the most damage with it, then bribe the ump again when it will screw them the most."

...St. Patrick, are you up there? Do you hear this?...

Ragtime then went on to inform me of an someone named 'Wally' who used to hang out at the bar with the Barflies. Unbeknownst to others, Wally was a Barfly himself, but was regularly called upon by the league to be an umpire. Basically an honest man, the league games gave him good reason to temporarily abandon his mores and accept the bribes whenever possible. Wally, unfortunatley, passed away a few years ago, but the Barflies fondly remember how he could be counted upon to pocket the cash whenever they called upon him.

The enthusiasm generated in Rick's is incredible. The whole crowd gets into the band act as musicians blow their hearts out to achieve heights they've perhaps never achieved before. Every night is a record-setter, and Ragtime Rick is right in the middle of it, beating the devil out of the piano as he looks for more notes to put into a tune:

'Somebody stole my gal...,'

...followed by two-fisted roaring up and down the keyboard to lead into the next line:

'Somebody stole my pal...,'

And when the tune finally comes to an end, Ragtime spins around on the piano stool grinning like a little kid, happy beyond words that he was able to have so much fun and share it with the customers. It was one such Saturday night when Richard Berry, ragtime player from West Bloomfield, stopped by Ragtime Rick's for a tomato sandwich.

Richard had to struggle to find a place to sit. The joint was packed wall to wall and everyone was having a great time. Ragtime and the band were thundering away at a furious pace on the bandstand, and now the waitress struggled between customers to take Richard's order.

"I'll have a tomato sandwich and a beer, please," he told her.

Her reply, to his everlasting astonishment, was:

"We got the sandwich, but no beer. Our license is temporarily suspended."

"What?!" blurted the amazed Richard, stuck in the middle of a place the rocked and vibrated in full sway to the music. *"What are all these people doing here if there's no beer?"*

"Well," she informed him, *"there was a government paperwork snafu. They claimed we didn't pay something that we paid and have receipts for, but the guys that were sent up here didn't have any authority to look at receipts. They left with our license and their office won't be open again until Tuesday, when Rick has to drive to Columbus to show the receipt to someone. So we're having a 'License Be Damned' party. Everyone's drinking Coke, coffee, and partying down."*

Richard watched in amazement as the band and Ragtime Rick roared into the next tune. Not even losing the liquor license for a few days could stop these guys from having a good time, and the syncopation thundered on as the waitress now slipped back through the din to bring him sliced tomatos on whole wheat, lettuce and mayonaise. And a complimentary Coke.

In 1986, the great ragtime/stride pianist Butch Thompson and his trio were scheduled to play a concert in Toledo. Knowing that the concert hall would be sold out, the Barflies bought a block of about 25 tickets. They arrived en masse at the concert hall in full regalia, blue jeans, orange Tee shirts and caps. This was immediately noticed by the tuxedoed ushers who were assigned to seat them, and now the Barflies entered the concert hall amid ladies in minks and evening gowns, men in tuxedos and concert-wear. The Barflies took their seats as assigned, constituting a huge orange block in the middle of the place. They drew stares, guffaws, and comments. One woman looked at them for a moment, turned away, and was heard to say 'Good God' to whoever she was with. The Barflies, undaunted, remained.

Butch was putting on a tremendous concert and now it had come to intermission. Ragtime Rick, accompanied by Duke Heitger, arose and went backstage to see Butch. They presented him with two gifts: one was the newest release of the Cakewalkin' Jass Band (courtesy of Ray Heitger) and the second was an orange Barfly shirt for Butch and each member of his band. Thompson thought this was hilarious, and he immediately removed his tuxedo jacket and pulled the Barfly shirt over his own shirt and bowtie. Then he returned to the concert stage to finish the second half. Ragtime and the Barflies were now being given thumbs-up by the surrounding misters and mavens, and they shouted and hooted their way through to the end of the concert. Butch Thompson, following the concert, then followed the Barflies back to Ragtime Rick's Saloon, where they partied and jammed until the wee hours of the morning, still wearing their orange shirts.

The list of craziness at Ragtime's is endless, but one of my favorite stories happened this way:

I had gone into Ragtime's to sit in, have a cup of coffee (I don't drink alcohol), and catch up on the latest insanity. And, true to form, there was insanity to report.

It seems that the previous night (a Wednesday) was a jam session. George, a gentlemen more senior than these raging counterparts, always came in during the afternoon and set up his drums for the session. Then he'd leave to return later. On this particular day, however, George was involved in a minor bicycle accident. He called Rick about six o'clock to inform him that he couldn't come back for the session. So now, when the jamming was about to begin, a set of drums was ready and waiting, but there was no one to play them.

Not to worry. A customer who'd come to listen volunteered that he could play the drums. This was fine with everyone, so now he took his place as the band prepared to begin. Then:

"Where's the drumsticks?" he asked.

Ragtime and the Undefeated Barflies quickly looked around. It appeared as if George intended to bring the sticks with him later, as he always did, so now they had to find something to give the drummer to replace the sticks. The Barflies had an idea:

"I'll bet there's something behind the bar that'll work," said one, and they all took off for the bar to find whatever it was they were looking for. It was useless, and twenty fruitless minutes went by. Perhaps the problem was that so many Barflies were behind the bar that they got in each other's way, but now the cook came out of the kitchen with a suggestion. He had two handfuls of spaghetti sticks. Could these possibly be of use? They might even sound like brushes.

One of the Barflies immediately wrapped grey tape around the stalks, and now the drummer was able to keep time with the band. A slight problem was that little pieces of spaghetti were rolling around on the drums, but that was minimal compared to having no drum at all. The spaghetti did indeed give a brush effect as he played, but by the end of the first set the improvised sticks were considerably shorter. The band now went on break.

It was during this break that a customer stood up and hailed one of the Barflies, most of whom had returned to their tables but some of whom were still searching behind the bar.

"Excuse me, sir," he said, waving across the room to them. *"Excuse me, sir, but do you suppose there might be some drum sticks in that case over there?"*

The Undefeated Barflies looked across the room to see what he was pointing at. It was a drum case (marked 'DRUMS'), sitting in plain sight (but out of sight from the drummer) near a table. George had left it earlier in the day. Upon opening the case, the Barflies discovered six sets of drum sticks, one of which they now proudly handed to their guest drummer. A gentleman, he thanked THEM for the sticks, not the customer. (He waited a moment until casting a sly wink to the customer, who in turn acknowledged it with subtlety.)

The Journeyman Piano Player sipped his coffee. He sat in with the band once or twice. He watched as, during the second break, Ragtime had to pull the entire hammer assembly out of the piano, grey-tape a hammer back together, replace a pin that had fallen out and disappeared into its bowels, and listen to stories from regular customers as to how certain moving components of the piano were fortified with parts made from tempered steel. And now, before Ragtime replaced the hammer rack, he ran up to the piano, sat down on the dilapidated stool, and started pulling a broken wire out of the thing. I watched him expertly replace it with a new one, 'field tune it,' (as we refer to emergency tunings), heave the hammer rack back into place, tighten it down with four bolts, and the band came back on stage to play on. Then Rick Graffing and the Undefeated Barflies roared off into another room-shaking rendition of some tune that was guaranteed to stick in your head for the next three weeks.

'Hello ma' baby, hello ma' honey, hello ma' ragtime gal...'

So if you go to Ragtime Rick's, enjoy yourself. Have a sandwich. Have a beer. Leave a tip on the table for the waitress, but leave a crowbar or wrench on the piano on your way out. They just might need it before the night is over.

And if they don't maybe the umpire does. And he just might be sitting at the bar with the Barflies watching you.

LET ED TAKE CHARGE

My old friend Ed had won the election and became the mayor of a town that I won't name. And, for the same reasons I can't name the town, you can assume also that his name isn't Ed. His campaign slogan, however, had been 'Let Ed Take Charge,' and the following two anecdotes should tell you in no uncertain terms that he meant what he said.

I was playing the piano in a saloon sometime between the years 1955 and 1990 when Ed would come in with his friends on a Friday night. They'd give me a friendly wave when the hostess took them to their booth, then sit down to begin the night's frivolity. On one such night, I had an obnoxious customer.

Some guy sitting close in front of the piano kept scowling at me. It didn't matter what I played, this guy couldn't be pleased. Even when Ed (a celebrity now) came across the room to say 'hi' to me and stop to chat, this character scowled on. It was after Ed returned to his booth that the character slowly arose and came up to me as I played. He stood glomming over me, imparting nervous tension as I wondered what he was going to say. But when I finished the tune, he didn't say anything. He just hovered there, like some ominous enforcer making his presence intimidating. When I started the next tune, I noticed that Ed was observing this guy. And now, the obnoxious one began to speak:

"You know," he began solemnly, *"and I know that you don't know how to play the piano."*

Then he turned and sat down again.

"What the hell does THAT mean?" I wondered. Apparently shaken, I noticed again that Ed was observing the proceedings. Ed could tell I was upset, and he wasn't smiling. About fifteen minutes later, the jerk arose again and returned to where I sat trying to make a living. His words weren't any better:

"I can hear that bullshit you call piano playing," he began, *"but I also know what real piano playing is. You can fool the people in this place, maybe, but you can't fool ME!"*

This time I quit in the middle of the tune. Being quite a few years younger than I am right now, I heated up and yelled something to this effect into his face:

"Jerks like you are the scum of the earth! You couldn't have a

good time if your grandmother paid you to do it, 'cause you wouldn't know how!"

The jerk retorted loudly, but his words were cut off suddenly. Ed had come out of his seat and had this guy by the lapels, yelling now point-blank into his face:

"LISTEN, ASSHOLE! I WANT YOU TO SHUT THE FUCK UP! WHEN YOU PISS OFF THE PIANO PLAYER, YOU PISS OFF ME!"

Then, turning to an astonished-looking piano player, he shouted:

"You want me to throw this jerk out of here, Bob? Go ahead and say so, if you do. I don't give a shit. I'll pitch him through the fuckin' door, if he's bothering you!"

I urged Ed to let go of this guy, convinced that there would be no further problem with him. The jerk returned to his table (and kept his mouth shut, finally leaving five minutes later) and Ed returned to his booth to keep a watchful eye on the matter.

When the obnoxious guest left, Ed later brushed off the incident, saying:

"Guys like that really piss me off."

Keeping in mind the campaign slogan 'Let Ed Take Charge', now read a second incident in which he most certainly did just that.

This one occurred at a different place in which I was playing. The diners and dancers had mostly gone home, and the hour was drawing late. I was finishing up some gentle listening music now and was preparing to take a break, and Ed was there again with several friends. Also, at a different table, sat a distinguished-looking man and woman. His gray hair was striking and his conservative suit bespoke a high ranking executive of some kind. I went over and said 'hello' to them on my break.

"We like this place," he mentioned. *"We are new in town, having just sold our house in Grosse Pointe to come out here, and we're pleased to have found such a pleasant establishment to come to."*

I did my best to welcome him to town, but now I saw Ed and his party laughing uproariously over something. I soon returned to the piano and began playing more easy listening. Then, it happened:

"Bob! Bob! Stop the music! Hold it a minute, will ya'?"

Ed was standing up at his table, waving his arms in the air and getting all his friends up with him.

"Out there," he yelled to them. *"Out there onto the dance floor, all of you!"*

Now he was shoving them onto the floor.

"Bob! Get away from the piano for a minute and join us!"

"Huh?", I questioned, but now Ed was rousing the executive and his wife out of their chairs as well.

"Hi, folks," he said. *"We want you to join us in having a little fun."*

The executive held his wife's hand as they were now pulled out onto the dance floor. Next, I was picked up and shoved in among them all.

"Everyone down on their knees," yelled Ed, and the puzzled expression on that executive's face is still clear in my mind as we were all now forced to kneel down in a circle on the dance floor. Ed then instructed that we lean forward, nose to nose, and clasp hands together. Thoughts of seances and camp voodoo whelmed up in by brain but, astonished as we all were, we followed his lead. Resembling pilgrims now, bowing to Mecca, we formed a noses down and rumps up ring-circle in the middle of this place. I imagined that the lights would now go off and ghastly images with lighting torches would enter from the wings. They didn't, of course, and now Ed was speaking in hushed tones, almost in solemnity:

"Repeat these words after me, everyone."

We cast nervous glances among ourselves before nodding agreement. The executive looked absolutely dumbstruck as Ed started his chant:

Ed: *"I know in my heart..."*
Us: *"I know in my heart..."*
Ed: *"and I know in my mind..."*
Us: *"and I know in my mind..."*
Ed: *"that all that's behind me..."*
Us: *"that all that's behind me..."*
Ed: *"is my big behind."*
Us: (rather slowly, and realizing we'd been had) *"...is my big behind."*

There we were, in a circle with our rumps up in the air and having just chanted *"all that's behind me is my big behind."* We'd been had gloriously, and Ed was smirking at us now across the floor.

His friends were beginning to giggle out of control. I didn't know what to think, and now I looked up at the executive who had an indescribable expression of disbelief on his face. I have never seen a more total look of amazement in my life, so I did the only thing I knew to facilitate the proceedings. I looked to him and said:

"Sir, did you say you were new in town?"

"Yes," he sighed. *"Yes, I did say that."*

"Well, sir," I continued, *"allow me to introduce you to the mayor of this town, Mr. Ed Smith. Ed, this man just sold his house in Grosse Pointe to move out here with us."*

"The mayor?" questioned the executive, his puzzled expression becoming more unbelievable with each passing second.

Still kneeling in the ring-circle, the men shook hands and made introductions. I slowly arose, found my jacket, and headed for the door. As I departed, I cast a quick glance back. There they were; grown men and women sitting and kneeling on the dance floor of an expensive restaurant, ostensibly discussing business, politics, and religion.

I left and went home.

THE BRONX PIANO PLAYER

People seem to have different reactions when they find someone sitting behind a piano bar. Those of us in this business find that most people, of course, recognize us as members of the human race, and have a natural amount of respect for us regardless of what we may sound like. Others, however, seem to have images of what we're supposed to be, and they can't let go of that image until they've made complete asses of themselves, and embarrassed us as well. Consider the following scenario:

I received a phone call to play in a place I'd never heard of. It was a neighborhood bar in one of the western suburbs of Detroit, and it was a rather nice place. Let's call it Al's Place. Al's had a nice grand piano, pleasant surroundings, and clientele that had been there for years. I would learn that many of these people had been coming to Al's regularly since the 1950's and, obviously, any new piano player was going to be an 'outsider,' as far as they were concerned. But since stuff like this is not unusual to Journeymen, (remember: Journeymen drive anywhere today to play any piano tonight...etc.) I didn't mind taking the job for a night.

My first set went fairly well. I played some slow standards, such as 'Deep Purple' and 'Mood Indigo,' and I mixed in a few slow rags as the people sat roughly thirty feet away at the bar. Although their backs were to me, I could see them casting glances in my direction by use of the mirror in back of the bar. Nonperturbed, I played on.

A friend of mine had come in to listen. Marv sat at a table alone, and whenever I'd play a rag, he'd perk up and smile. I know that Marv likes ragtime and doesn't really go for piano bar atmospheres, so I'd try to work in a few here and there to let him know that his trip had been worthwhile. He appreciated it and signaled a friendly gesture from time to time.

I generally play long sets. Sometimes piano bars become a lot of fun for everyone, and I'll end up playing two or three hours at once. Therefore, I didn't think it unusual after I'd been playing for an hour to these people. I was playing a businessman's bounce tempo to 'The Hawaiian War Chant' when some woman suddenly turned on her barstool, jumped off, and came running in my direction. I looked up and smiled.

"Hey!" she yelled, seemingly offended by something. *"When ya*

gonna shut up so we can play the jukebox?"

I politely informed her that I would end the tune in progress and take a break. She grimaced and began fumbling around in her purse for some quarters. And as the 'Hawaiian War Chant' came to an end, the sound of Bill Haley singing 'Rock Around The Clock' erupted from the jukebox.

"Hmm," thought the Journeyman. *"They like 50's music."*

A few people came over to the piano that night. They were nice, and they liked to sing along to some of the tunes as well. One of them showed me how to turn on the microphone so they could sing into it. Cringing, I watched as a lady pointed out the various switches and dials connecting a decrepit microphone on a cord that hung across the keyboard to any customer who felt like singing. I smiled and thanked her for showing it to me.

If there is anything that can destroy a piano job, it is a microphone for the customers. They all know each other. They've grown up together. They've drank in the same bar for, in this case, decades together, and the piano player is someone who had better know their tunes in the keys they want to sing them or there's going to be a lot of uncomfortable moments before the night is through. So, as previously stated, I cringed, smiled, and thanked her when she showed me the microphone.

The lady who had shown me this microphone was very pleasant, nearing seventy years of age (I'd guess), and now she wanted to sing the next tune. She was actually quite good and I enjoyed playing it as she sang in that beautiful, slow tempo that gives feeling and purpose to a song. Everyone, including myself, applauded when she was done, and I asked her to sing another one. She agreed, and we played and sang together the old classic 'How Soon.' The customers loved it, I loved it, and now I could see the jukebox woman staring across the room at me again. I suggested to the lady at the piano that we take a short break, which we did.

As I arose from the bench, 'You Ain't Nothin' But A Houn'dog' suddenly busted loose from the glowing, blinking juke box machine against the wall. The juke lady was boogying across the floor, and I walked toward the bar to get a Coke. My thoughts consisted of trying to recall the barmaid's name (this was my first night there), thinking about how pleasantly the lady at the piano had been singing, and thinking about the soon-to-arrive problems with any microphone around a piano bar, when I suddenly was confronted by some character who stood about five-foot two-inches and was scowling into my face.

This elderly man, and I don't say this to be mean, resembled a troll. He was short, gaunt, gnarled, wrinkled, and wore heavy horn-rim glasses through which he glared up into my face. Before I could utter a word, he said:

"Listen, kid, I've got all the authority in this place. I've been drinking here longer than any of these people, and I'm gonna tell you right now that if you don't play dance music, your butt'll be outa' here in no time."

"Huh?" I managed.

"You sit over there playin' all that woosie-goosi crap for her to sing," he continued, *"and neither of you can hold a tempo worth a damn. No one would get up and dance to that garbage you're playing 'cause you speed up, slow down, speed up, slow down. And that RAGTIME you play, forget it. It don't go in this place. So I'm telling you now - BECAUSE I LIKE YOU, KID - to either play dance music AND PLAY IT GOOD, or get the hell out of here."*

With that, he returned to his bar stool.

I quietly picked up my Coke and just as quietly tried to be inconspicuous as the jukebox now roared out a hillbilly classic from the 50's:

> *'See the big eight-wheeler goin' down the track,*
> *Means your true-lovin' daddy ain't comin' back*
> *He's movin' on...'*

Watching the jukebox woman spinning and gyrating on the dance floor gave me the impression that these people did indeed like to dance, and I was now in the position of trying to let people sing, dance, or listen, and keep them all happy.

"Hmm," thought the Journeyman, noting that Marv had gotten up and left. *"Not too simple."*

'All The Authority' sat at the far end of the bar as I started my next set, for which I was thankful. *"The farther away from him, the better,"* I thought. I looked up to see that my friend Florence had come in. She is a fine musician and is very aware of the perils befalling piano bars. She winked and gave me the 'thumbs up' sign. Smiling weakly, I began playing 'Misty' in a steady dance tempo, and when I was half-way through it I looked up to see a second elderly woman had come over from the bar and was standing next to me. She was smiling profoundly, holding the microphone in her hands already, and she said to me, in a low whisper:

"Oh, hi there. Everyone wants to hear me sing 'Blue Moon.'"

Since I was only a few choruses into 'Misty,' I tried to gauge how long to play the tune for anyone wanting to dance. 'All The Authority' sat with his back to me not even acknowledging that I was there, and I quickly looked at the other customers to see if any of them were on the verge of dancing. The lady on my left now leaned down to say:

"You know 'Blue Moon,' don't you?"

Then, singing into my ear as I tried to keep the beat to 'Misty:'

"Blue Moon, you saw me standing alone..."

'All The Authority' sat silently on his barstool, and more friends of mine were drifting in. Walter is a retired editor of a major newspaper and has appeared at many elegant restaurants over the years to enjoy fine dining and listen to ragtime. He'd heard that I would be playing at Al's and had brought some of his journalism friends with him that night. Dressed immaculately in suits and ties, they took several tables in the middle of this neighborhood bar. So hoping against hope that everything would go smoothly for the most influential press corps in town, I ended 'Misty' and started thinking about 'Blue Moon.' But before I even had a chance to find out what key, what tempo, what anything, the woman next to me was already singing it into the microphone. I fumbled around, found the key, and tried to catch up with her:

"...without a dream in my heart,
Without a love of my own..."

An incredible thing was happening, however. This woman couldn't keep a beat. She would sing 3, 4, 5, or even 6 beats into a measure. All thought of dancing was out the window, and I watched as 'All The Authority' sat glomming off into the distance thinking dark thoughts beyond my imagination as we agonized our way through the tune. 'Blue Moon' sounded something like this:

"Blue Moon" - (pause, pause, 'why the hell doesn't she sing the next note? - pause, pause. Then, finally...) *"Now I'm..."* (Good Lord! Why's she holding 'I'm' so long? Hurry up, woman! Hurry up!)

"*...no longer alone, now I'm no longer alone...*" (No, for God's sake! No! You're singing the same words all over again!) "*...without a dream in my heart...*" (Whew! She ended. What? Oh, NO!)... "*without a love of my own.*" (I can't believe it! She invented a whole phrase and put it into the end of the tune! How the hell...)

And now, dear reader, she was going into another verse. The woman smiled to everyone and motioned that I was going to play a few bars before she came in singing again. It was then that I suddenly felt like the Bronx piano player.

"*The 'Bronx piano player?'*" you ask.

Well, yes, and here is what 'the Bronx piano player' is all about.

There's an old joke, known among piano players, about the guy who got a job playing piano in some Mafia joint in the Bronx. One night, the owner walks up to him, bringing a built-like-bull hoodlum in tow. The owner announces to the piano player:

"*Mr. Piano Player, my friend Vito wants to sing 'Strangers In The Night.' You will play it for him, yes?*"

"*Uh, yes,*" mumbles the piano player, looking up at some street-tough plug-ugly. "*Sure. Why not.*"

"*Excellent, Mr. Piano Player,*" says the owner, now adding, "*but there is one thing you must do, sir. Vito, he likes to sing in 5/4 time. Do that for him, will you? Thanks.*"

"*Five-four time?*" questions the piano player. "*Uh, how do you play 'Strangers In...'*"

"*Just do it!*" snaps the owner. Then, turning and beaming to the his guests and patrons:

"*Vito, SING FOR THE WONDERFUL PEOPLE, NOW!*"

The piano player plays a few nervous chords as the hood draws himself up gracelessly next to the piano, arms stiff at his sides. When the piano introduction is over, Vito opens his mouth and sings:

"*Strangers in da fuckin' night...*"

Well, do you get the idea? There I was, with 'All The Authority' sitting at one end of the place, some woman glaring at me to take a break so she could play the jukebox, dancers presumedly too irate to get up from their barstools and head for the dancefloor, and I sat there like the Bronx Piano Player while some maven chortled out 'Blue Moon' in 5/4, 6/4, and 7/4 time. I looked up at Florence, mouthed the word 'Vito,' and she broke up laughing. I also noticed - "*Oh, no!*" -

Walter, the newspaper editor, was heading for the door! Strange, though; his friends all remained at the tables.

But there was more craziness to unfold before the Bronx, uh, the Journeyman Piano Player would escape Al's that night. My friend Richard Berry had just walked in and sat down at the piano bar. He would soon be wishing that he hadn't.

Richard Berry is a fine ragtime pianist. He is not, however, a professional pianist. Richard is a software engineer for a major Detroit auto manufacturer and can 'play the computer' like any virtuoso can play the piano. In many ways, I am envious of people like Richard. They don't have to go out and endure the stuff that I have to go through trying to make a living in this business. Richard, for example, has a beautiful seven-foot grand piano in his house to learn and practice on, unlike the two old uprights I have but learn little from. I learn tunes from tapes while 'on the fly' between jobs.

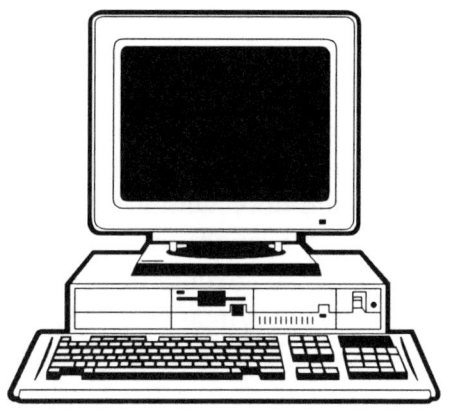

Richard has been featured at many ragtime festivals as a guest artist, and his delicate, lilting style is always a highlight on any program. So now, I looked up to see Richard Berry, gentleman, soft-spoken, honors graduate from M.I.T., sitting in Al's Place as I struggled to get through the night. Finally, I had a brainstorm.

"Ladies and gentlemen," I announced over the P.A. system, "we are very fortunate tonight to have Richard Berry joining us. He is a featured ragtime pianist across the country, and I'm sure we can get him to play a few Scott Joplin tunes for us now."

There was polite applause (and a LOT of applause from Walter's table) as Richard approached the piano. I took a break and headed for the bar again. Another Coke sounded pretty good to me at the moment, and now I could hear the beautiful strains from Joplin's 'Harmony Club Waltz' drifting among the conversations in the room. I cast a quick glance toward 'All The Authority,' and he hadn't moved from his back-turned position, staring away from us all.

I stopped by Walter's table to talk to his wife, Liz, and their friends.

"Where'd Walt go?" I asked.

"Oh," explained Liz. "We brought all these people here for dinner when we heard you'd be here, but this place doesn't have a menu."

"What?!" I replied. "You must be kidding. They don't have any food here?"

"No," continued Liz, "so we asked the waitress if she'd bring us some paper plates, plastic forks, and napkins..."

I quickly glanced around to see that everyone had these classic picnic items situated in front of them as Liz continued:

"...and Walt - Oh! Here he comes now!"

I looked up to see one of the most distinguished men in the field of journalism, elegant in his dapper suit and horn-rim glasses, coming through the door with a stack of pizzas in boxes for his guests, all of whom he'd brought to hear me play the piano.

"Hi, Bob," exclaimed Walt cheerfully. "Want some pizza?"

The Journeyman Piano Player got up from the table and pursued the Coke he'd originally been seeking. Standing at the bar, I had to wait a few moments for the barmaid. She was scurrying to keep up with the waitresses, and now she finally ran up to me.

"Coke, Bob?" she asked, and I nodded to her, also listening to the beautiful melodies coming through the room as Richard so delicately stroked the keys. Walter and his friends were enjoying fine dining from open pizza boxes at their tables, and they had little plastic containers of additional anchovies and heated mushrooms to put on their dinners. I watched as one man sprinkled mushrooms into the box to enhance the evening's meal. Now the barmaid was back.

"How much do I owe you?" I asked, knowing that she'd decline any money from an employee. As she good-naturedly waved off the cash, I noticed that the piano music had stopped.

"How'd that happen?" I wondered. I'd been waiting for one of my favorite strains to come up as the tune closed, but I hadn't heard it. So I picked up the Coke and went back towards the piano. There I found Richard. He'd stopped playing and was leaning back on the piano bench because some drunk, beer in hand, had bent over to stare straight into his face as he roared - loudly - to Richard:

"WHAT DO YOU MEAN YOU DON'T KNOW 'SUMMERTIME?' I WANT TO SING IT!"

As I stood looking, in horror, the drunk was now yelling into

Richard's face:

"EVERYONE KNOWS 'SUMMERTIME!' COME ON, YOU MUST KNOW IT..."

Then, blasting out the first three notes of Gershwin's classic tune, the drunk with all his beery breath bellowed straight into Richard's face:

"SUM - mer - TIIIIMMEE...."

I tapped the drunk on the shoulder. When he looked up at me, I asked Richard if he needed help, and he agreed that he did. He quickly got off the piano bench, my two-minute break came to an end, and I began playing 'Summertime' as the drunk now picked up the microphone and belted it out, smiling and emoting as he went. He was happy, now. Richard commented to me later:

"Bob; I've never smelled such foul breath in my life."

This was a one-night job that I played, and I've often wondered what 'All The Authority' thought of this. He scowled all night, unable to resolve the simplest problem, while Walter and the press corps, conversely, laughed and had a good time. They couldn't be stopped even by a place that had no menu.

I also wonder if 'All The Authority' sings 'Strangers In The Night."

A NIGHT IN THE DITCH

Bill Roper was an amazing clarinet player. He was also a colorful character in his thick black hair and Captain Ahab beard. Although a tragic disease took him from us in the early 1990's, his playing and bizarre legacy will be talked about for years. Consider the following story:

Roper had been playing at some mansion for a Dixieland buffet brunch that lasted well into the evening. The band was allowed to eat and drink whatever and all that they wanted. That was a mistake, but by the time the hostess realized the mistake it was too late to do anything about it.

The hostess asked the band if they wanted to take any of the leftovers from the buffet with them. There was corned beef, chicken salad, and the like to select from. Roper put a few things into tin-foil wrappers, politely thanked her, and departed. So far, so good, but this is when the chaos started.

Roper and someone who wants to remain anonymous got into a Volkswagen beetle to make their escape. Careening through the city streets until they reached the interstate expressway, they now entered the cloverleaf entrance ramp at pole-sitter speed. Roaring out onto the throughway as though it were the far turn at the Indy 500, the Volkswagen suddenly went lurching out of control as they discovered their reflexes weren't as quick as anticipated. And now, of course, the Volkswagen beetle was rolling over and over down the median strip as they proved to all they were too smashed to drive the thing.

Cars came to screeching halts at the same time the beetle was ending up on its roof amid great clouds of dust. People were running all over the expressway in the early dusk as Roper and Anonymous crawled out the windows. With Roper now standing, albeit somewhat dazed, someone ran up to him and said:

"Are you all right, buddy?" And then, with a horrified *"Aarghh!,"* the same guy turned around and ran back to his car. Then a woman ran up to him:

"Are you - ohmagawd!"

She likewise turned around and ran.

Roper stumbled around for several minutes, and he noticed now that people were shunning him overtly. Finally, a policeman arrived. His opening line was:

"Excuse me sir, but - OH, JESUS!"

Now the cops were telling him to take it easy, sit down, and the ambulance will be right here.

"I don't need an ambulance," vehemently replied our clarinet player. *"I'm fine!"*

The cops told him to sit down, lean back against the Volkswagen, and relax. Finally, he did. Then, in the middle of the expressway median with people lining both sides of the road from a safe distance, Roper reached up to scratch his head. He found it. The corned beef was stuck in his thick black hair, protruding upwards as if his brains were coming out of his head.

No one watching could understand how some guy could be sitting out in the median, propped up against the inverted wreckage, and laughing hysterically to himself as cars and eighteen-wheelers went roaring by. They must have thought it was the final act of a brain-damaged crash victim, but no one wanted to get close enough to find out.

Bill Roper with Bob Milne and Lynn 'See you on the piano bench' Evans
Photo courtesy of a special fan

'WHEN IRISH EYES ARE SMIiii - LING...'

St. Patrick's Day is always approached with some trepidation by most piano players. Although I love the true Irish music, and have even assisted on some recordings of the great Irish balladeer Charley Taylor, I know in advance that every crackpot in the area is going to get drunk and pretend to be Irish on St. Patrick's Day. They come from out of the woodwork to suddenly develop a 'brogue,' talk in glowing terms about the Emerald Isle as if they actually knew something about it, and down the pints at the bar as if they're accustomed to doing so. They're not.

I recall an incident at the Rathskeller bar many years ago between a phony 'Irishman' with a shillelagh, a bartender, and a genuine Irishman who refused to get drunk on St. Patrick's Day. The Irishman also informed me, in almost reverent tones, that St. Patrick's is a quiet day in Ireland. It is not given over to drunkards. The conversation opens with the drunk, dressed in fitted three-piece suit, hatted, and acting like landed gentry, hailing the bartender:

Drunk: "Aye, me laddie! Give us all a round of stout!"

Bartender: *"That's quite a shillelagh you have there, Mr. Ball. Is it from Ireland?"*

Drunk: *"Aye, it 'tis, me bucko! It comes from the Highlands!"*

Genuine Irishman: *"Where abouts in the Highlands?"*

Drunk: (suddenly looking puzzled, after a pause) *"Like I said, it comes from the Highlands. Barkeep! More stout!"*

Genuine Irishman: (repeating) *"I said - WHERE ABOUTS IN THE HIGHLANDS?"*

Drunk: (taking the offensive) *"If ye 'er Irish, ye aughta' know from lookin' at it; eh, me laddie? Ha-ha! HA-HA! 'Tis a shillelagh from the Highlands!"*

Genuine Irishman: (becoming furious) *"You're a bullshitter!"*

Drunk: (becoming dramatic and acting astonished) *"ME? A bullshitter? You are accusing ME, my good man, of slinging the bull?"*

Genuine Irishman: (his voice raising as he now raved to the entire bar) *"I say to you, and I say to this whole place, that if you can't tell me where in the Highlands that shillelagh came from, then you're a bullshitter! Do you hear? I say to you, sir, YOU ARE A BULLSHITTER!"*

The drunk looked longingly at the shillelagh. A tear seemed to appear in his eye. Finally, in heart-rending tones and almost weeping, he stage-whispered to the genuine Irishman:

"Ye ask me 'where in the Highlands did it come from.' Well, I must tell ye sir, and I mean this from the bottom of me heart - me gran-pappy never told me."

"BULLSHIT!" yelled the Irishman, as he brought his fists down on the bar. *"YOU ARE, SIR, FILLED WITH BULLSHIT!"*

He then turned and stormed out the door, leaving us to deal with this imbecile. As I eased back toward the piano I could hear the drunk, in full magniloquence and brogue, continuing now on the poor captive bartender:

"A bullshitter, am I? Heh, heh; well, just look at the gnarled burls in this old shillelagh, me bucko. It grew near the banks of the River Shannon and it's clubbed a few heads in a few pubs, I'll tell ye! Yes, there's a rich heritage that comes with this old relic of the Isle. Let me tell ye 'bout the time me gran-pappy went to town with it. It was on a Friday night in Cork..."

The bartender, professional that he was, actually stood listening with a straight face. He knew, like everyone else, that there are no 'Highlands' in Ireland. The Highlands are in Scotland.

Just as bad, if not worse, than phony Irishmen is the desire for these guys to sing the same songs over and over and over again. 'When Irish Eyes Are Smiling,' although it alludes to the Irish, was written by a New York songwriter who had never set foot in Ireland. This is similar to the fact that when Stephen Foster was looking for a name of some place to follow the line 'Way down upon the _____,' he consulted a map of someplace south. He happened to pick up Florida. 'Okefenokee,' 'Chattahoochee,' and 'Lake Okeechobee' didn't seem to fit either the idea or the music, so he finally decided (right off the map) on 'Suwanee River,' which originates in Okefenokee Swamp. With a stroke of genius, he copied the letters, matched the syllables to his tune, and Voila! - another masterpiece was born. Fortunately, his masterpiece is not given over the way 'Irish Eyes' is every March to some idiot, his hands clutched together as he emotes his way toward the high note, and the ultimate splattering of same. Anthropologists will surely add 'Homo Bozo' to the ranks at some point in time to commemorate this otherwise unbelievable ritual.

In an attempt at self defense, I once wrote an insane version of an 'Irish Ballad' that I'd perform from time to time. When the crap became too thick, I'd simply sing 'Six Rollicking Lads.' When it was over, there would inevitably be dead silence. Following would be a pause of perhaps half an hour before anyone wanted me to do anything 'Irish' again. The wily journeyman had managed to kill a substantial part of the clock getting through a rough barroom night, and hastened the onset of the after-gig coffee shop. There could be found the welcome relief of the crossword puzzle.

And silence. And silence...

Six Rollicking Lads

Six rollicking lads from county Dare
They found an old woman in a wheel chair
"Let's give her the fling from the bridge right there"
And the others replied with "Good cheer, good cheer!"

So, over the rail, (they were young, full of spice!)
She ricocheted up, ("Going once! Going twice!")
From off the froze water she bounced, ("Going thrice!")
till she stove in the surface and crashed through the ice,
Singin' "HEY, DERRY DERRY, DOWN DOWN!"

Chorus:
Oh, down, down, singin' hey derry down,
Singin' hey derry derry, down down!

"Good flinging!" cried one, and they all danced around,
They whistled and sang and skipped over the ground,
Hoisting their ales and swilling them down
They were watched by a man, and he scowled and
frowned...

For there stood the sheriff, his thumbs in his britches,
With longbows they hid in the gulleys and ditches
The crossbow was cranked 'till it strained at its' winches
And he spoke to his men...
"SHOOT THE SONS OF BITCHES!"
(Oh down, derry derry, down down!)

So, high in the air, like the soaring of sparrows,
Across the wide fields filled with plowshafts and harrows
Then down on the bridge, where the deep water narrows
Came feathers and shafts and a hail of arrows,
(GOOD GOD! derry derry, down down!)

One, shot through the brains, floated off to the sea,
Another resembled a bramble-bush tree,
And spinning, was one, like a windmill, while three
Hung like pendulums skewered to the bridge, "YIPPEE!
(yelled the sheriff, just bursting with glee!)

"Good Shooting!" said he, and they ran pell mell
To pick up the ale from the ground where it fell
"GOOD BEER! GOOD BEER!" they were all heard to yell,
What a hell of a tale to tell, to tell,
What a hell of a tale to tell.

So, off they went singin' "Hey down derry derry"
Their song, on the wind, to the village did carry
Where they found an old woman on crutches, "Let's tarry!"
"Will ye no cross the bridge with us, Ma'am', and make merry?"
Singin' "HEY, DERRY DERRY DOWN DOWN!"

Oh, "Down down," singin' "Hey derry down!"
They whistled and carried her high o'er the ground
And a hole in the ice 'neath the bridge can be found,
Singin' "Hey, derry derry, down down, down down,"
Singin'

"HEY, DERRY DERRY, DOWN DOWN!"

End

"HELLO, BOB. WE'VE BEEN OUT 'TIPPING' TONIGHT..."

For some reason, I feel that I need to remind the reader before relating this tale, that all the stories in this book are true. I find myself, when I think back on this one, wondering if this was some mutant dream from the quasi-zone that somehow got stuck in my mind, but the two characters involved are life-long friends of mine and I confirmed the details of this wild event before putting it into print. You'll understand, of course, that I can't use their real names here.

I have known John and Bill all my life. They are slightly older than I, but the three of us grew up together. Therefore, I am aware of the underlying cause in the following tale; ego.

Ego, the need to prove oneself, is something we all have to contend with, and it seems that when we're younger, the drive is stronger. I can distinctly remember when an older student in the music school, John Thyson was his name, took me aside on day and said:

"Bob, play the horn to the best of your ability. Be the best you can, but don't try to be the best in the world. There's no such thing."

I couldn't believe what I was hearing, and the echo of that last line has been in my head for thirty years now - "There's no such thing!"

That advice didn't make any sense to me in my late teens, but I also distinctly remember when it finally did make sense. The best music I ever heard was played by people who had nothing to prove. I was older now, and I realized that there is no such thing as 'the best' in the field of arts.

At any rate, my friends John and Bill were rivals, in a nice way. They are both extremely intelligent, both having genius-level IQs. (John has a near 100% photographic memory). They were both, at the time, extremely strong physically. Bill is six-foot seven-inch and possessed awesome strength while John, and six-foot two-inch, trained in gyms to develop similar strength.

Besides their strength, they were then, and are now, highly respected in their fields. Bill is a self-made multi-millionaire and John is a leading research scientist. I add this to tell you that the characters in this story are not barroom rum-dummies, bent on winning the next arm-wrestling contest. These are class citizens, both of whom possessed an ego to lead us into the following scene. Oh well; here goes:

I was playing piano in the Rathskeller, sometime around 1970, when John and Bill came in. They were dressed nicely in shirts and ties, looking chipper, and when I took a break I went and sat with them. Bill looked up at me with a mirthful smirk and said in his deep, resonant voice:

"Hello, Bob. We've been out tipping tonight."

My first thought, as yours probably is, was that they were out 'tipping a few beers tonight,' but I also saw John laugh slightly under his breath to Bill's statement. I looked to Bill and said:

"Having a few beers, are you? Sounds like fun."

But he answered:

"Well, yeah, that too. But actually, Bob, we're just out 'tipping' tonight," and they smirked to each other again.

Now I can tell you readers that they hadn't been tipping too many beers, because I have seen these guys in action before. I have seen Bill get into a drinking contest with some guy who called himself 'the drinking champion of the Pacific Fleet,' and when it was over, Bill was standing in the Rathskeller (all 6'7" of him) with the fleet champion lying passed out on the barroom table. Then I watched Bill (by now drunk, of course,) spread his arms wide open, flit his eyes across all the ladies in the room, and roar to the everlasting astonishment:

"I have defeated the champion of the Pacific Fleet, and now I have a quart of sperm in me!"

As John and others tried to drag him out the door, he continued ranting descriptive phrases to specific females as to how they could help alleviate the dire 'quart of sperm' problem he was dealing with. A stunned-into-silence room full of men with their wives and dates watched stone-faced as they dragged Bill out the door. Therefore, with Bill now sitting across the table from me nonchalantly mentioning they'd been out 'tipping,' I knew it wasn't some kind of wild, drunken activity he was referring to. He was too calm. Finally, cautiously, I asked:

"Tipping, Bill? Are you out, uh, leaving big tips for waiters, or something like that?"

(Since Bill was and still is a multi-millionaire, he does like to leave nice gratuities for deserving people. His basic nature is very generous). But instead, he smirked to John:

"No, Bob; we're just out, uh, 'tipping.' That's all. Just 'tipping.' Heh, heh."

I returned to the piano and played another set, wondering all the while just what the hell these guys had gone and done this time. I can remember when Bill returned a steak because it was over-cooked. The chef, (assuming a lofty attitude toward an 'insulant' customer) sent out a raw steak in return. Bill, however, took the incident seriously, picked up the steak, walked back into the kitchen with it, and beat the chef over the head and body with the thing as he simultaneously explained to the clown that he'd picked the wrong customer to insult. (Try to imagine a 6'7" healthy male coming through the door with a steak in his hands to assail you with.)

So I played all kinds of scenarios in my head over what this 'tipping' thing might be about. Returning after my next break, I was told the news.

John spoke up:

"Bob; you know where the King Lounge is?"

"Of course," I answered. *"It's one of my favorite corned beef places out on Woodward Avenue."*

"Well," he continued, *"Bill and I went there tonight for a corned beef and a beer. Bill was driving, and when we pulled up to angle park in front, some hot-dog in a Nash darted into the parking place right in front of us. Our car was rocking on its springs from having to brake so hard."*

"Hmm," I ventured. *"Very rude of him."*

I saw Bill laughing under his breath. Since I was aware how Bill has handled rude people in the past, (the steak incident) I was naturally curious. John continued:

"Bill blew the horn at him, but the dude jumped out of his car, flipped us the bird, and ran in the door."

I was beginning to sense something ominous here, because I have never known anyone to 'flip the bird' to these guys and get away with it, so I let John keep talking:

"We parked the car around the corner and ran back to get in," he said, *"and you know what happened? The same dude was coming out of the john, elbowed his way in front of us to get in line first, and they seated him at a table while Bill and I had to stand at the fucking door."*

I could tell, from the turn in the language, that they were displeased with having to 'stand by the fucking door' for this character, and my knowledge of their past history of dealing with such matters was generating a horrible, uncomfortable feeling in me. Trying to act at ease, I asked:

"What happened?"

Bill looked up and said, mellifluously:

"Oh, nothing, Bob. Nothing at all."

After a moment of silence, John looked at me and said:

"Bill called the maitre d', slipped him a fiver, and told him that we were with the gentleman sitting by himself. The maitre d' said 'come with me, gentlemen,' took us through the room, and seated us at the same table with the dude."

I was starting to develop great fears and trepidations, wondering, "these guys went and sat down at the same table with this jerk who'd cut them off and flipped them the bird?" Now, Bill continued with this wild story:

"Oh, it was nothing, Bob. The maitre d' seated us with him, we smiled and said 'Thank you for so generously sharing your table with us,' and after putting him at ease, we hailed the waiter."

John took over now:

"Yeah; the waiter came over and took our orders. Bill told him to 'get this guy the best steak in the house,' and we all struck up a conversation. The guy apologized for stealing the parking place and giving us the finger, and we just laughed it off. We bought him drinks, had dinner with him, Bill put his arm around him at one point as a gesture of friendship, and we sat in there for two hours drinking, laughing, and having a good time."

John stopped talking here, but I knew it wasn't over. These guys don't sit and yuk it up with people who treat them like this, and now Bill was adding:

"That's right, Bob. We had a great dinner with him. Then we hailed the waiter for dessert. The guy ordered a sundae."

"What did you order," I asked.

"Oh, nothing," replied Bill. "I picked up the tab and told him we had to leave. We were going 'tipping.'"

"Oh, Lord - here it comes," I thought. I was right. John was talking now:

"Yeah; the waiter brought the sundae, we slapped the dude on the back, got up, went out front, and tipped his fucking car up on its side."

"WHAT???!!!" I blurted. "WHAT DID YOU SAY???!!!"

Keep in mind, dear reader, that these two characters were talking to me with slightly more excitement than if they'd been describing an afternoon at the beach. And now, with the afore-mentioned ego problems in mind, read on as John calmly related the rest of this to me:

"Yeah," he said, "it was kind of strange. Somehow or other, without us ever talking about it, we both knew that we were going to get up from that table, go out front, and stand his car on its side. When Bill looked up and said 'we were going tipping,' we both already knew what we were going to do."

Now Bill added:

"But I didn't want John to hurt himself."

"Hurt yourself?" I puzzled.

"Yeah," said John. "When we got outside, the biggest problem we had was 'which one of us was going to do it.' Bill said, 'I want to do it,' and I told him, 'Bullshit! You're not strong enough to do it!' And Bill said, 'Bullshit, yourself! I'm twice as strong as you are, you twerp. Watch this.' And he reached down, grabbed the thing by its rocker panel, and tipped it up on its side."

I was sitting there in shock, not knowing what to say. Bill was calmly looking around the Rathskeller and sipping a beer as this conversation took place, but now John was adding:

"He didn't get it all the way, though. He got it all the way up on its side, but it wouldn't stay put. It took both of us to wiggle it back and forth to keep the thing from falling back on its wheels."

Bill was still, incredibly, just looking around the Rathskeller, hardly concerned at all with what was being said. And now, John was adding the final details:

"Oil came pouring out of the engine and was running all over the parking lot, and I heard the door handle when it popped into the door. Then there was this god-awful smell of gas, and we took off running."

The Journeyman Piano Player had great difficulty playing the piano for the rest of that night. John and Bill eventually got up and left, stopping by the piano to say 'good night.' But later, I conducted my own little follow-up to this story.

The next night, I stopped by the King Lounge to eavesdrop. I learned the following details from a waiter:

The previous night, everyone looked up to the sounds of sirens and flashing lights outside. Both the police and fire departments were in the parking lot. Some customer got up from his sundae, went outside to see what the commotion was, and found his car standing on its side surrounded by police and hosemen. Gasoline had run out the fill-pipe, all over the parking lot, and out into Woodward Avenue. It required several hours to clear the gas, and two wreckers to get the thing back onto its wheels and haul it away when the police were done with it.

A BOLT FROM THE BLUE

In about three hours, I would be leaving for Toledo. It was early summer, June 2, 1987, to be precise, and the 120-mile drive was routine by now. I'd been driving it for three years already, and spent the time in the car learning new tunes, dreaming up new pieces of music, or composing poems to myself. But first, I had some errands to run in town.

I was playing piano five nights a week and running a small sawmill part-time at my deep-in-the-woods house, located about seven miles northwest of Lapeer, Michigan. I can drive the back-country roads between my place and town blindfolded if necessary. The approaching thunderstorm boomed in the distance, and the sick-yellow color of the sky meant nothing unless someone happened to be up in an airplane, so I jumped in the car, snapped on the radio news station and began thinking about what would be the fastest order to run the errands:

"Let's see; if I go to the store first, then the ice cream might be melted by the time I get back. O.K., I'll do that last. First, it'll be the tire store to drop off this flat, then the bank, then the office supply for the printer ribbon for the book I'm working on, then..."

Leaning against the door as I relaxed, I looked to my left past a large maple tree to see three men standing in the doorway of an open barn. The large raindrops starting to hit my windshield indicated they were doing a wise thing, and I returned to thinking about errands:

"Maybe I should stop at the card shop first..."

Thats' when I felt my car being blasted to the side of the road, as if some ghastly force had the entire vehicle in its grip, choking and shaking it like a rag doll in the hand of King Kong. A blinding white flash around me was more brilliant than anything I can describe, and the next thing I remember is sitting in a stopped car in the middle of the road wondering what happened.

"I couldn't have been hit by lightning," I thought, *"Or I'd be dead. They measure that stuff in millions of volts."*

Then, I decided that lightning must have hit near me, perhaps the tree by the road where I saw the men in the barn. Now, suddenly feeling fear from the nearness of the strike, I thought I should get back home, about three miles backwards, so I turned the car around and went racing back up the road. The three men watched me go flying by.

But now, I decided that lightning probably doesn't hit in the same place twice, so it was probably all right to go back into town. I turned the car around again, and went racing now for town. The sooner I could get there, the better, and the three men stood watching as I flew by their barn again.

I repeated this manuever four or five times, literally driving in circles within a half-mile stretch of the road, and the men continued watching me. Finally, I drove up to their barn to see if they knew where the lightning had struck.

"It struck right thar', buddy," said one, pointing to the maple tree near the road. I looked at the tree to see absolutely no damage to it, still not realizing that the man was pointing to where my car had been. Then he said to me:

"You feel all right, mister?"

"Yeah, I'm fine," I added. Then I took off once again for town.

After arriving on the main street of Lapeer, I stopped at my usual spot to go to the Post Office first. I went inside and discovered I had no mail that day, and would later learn the reason why: I'd already been to the Post Office that day and had picked up the mail earlier. I just didn't remember it. Returning to my car to run the next errand, I didn't have the foggiest idea what I was supposed to be doing in town. Now, with rain coming down in torrents, I snapped on the radio to hear what the news station had to say about tornadoes, perhaps. I twisted the dial a few times 'on' and 'off,' but there was no sound, and when I looked out the window to see the aerial blackened and hanging in shreds, it still didn't occur to me why there was no sound coming from the radio: it was fried, and the funny smell coming from the dashboard was actually coming from the radio's melted parts.

"I wonder how close I was to that lightning," I wondered, and was beginning to notice that my left shoulder and elbow were starting to hurt. I also wondered why I was in town, and finally spotted the bankbook on the seat next to me.

"Oh, yeah, I was supposed to go to the bank," I thought, and now headed down the street to the bank.

I ran inside amidst thunder and downpour, and the teller finally asked me:

"Are you all right, Mr. Milne? You don't seem to know why you're here."

I laughed about *"just being hit by lightning,"* and every teller in the place came down to tell me to go to the hospital.

"Why?" I said. *"It didn't kill me, so there's nothing to fear now."*

By now, my shoulder and elbow were beginning to throb violently. I hadn't realized yet that I'd been leaning against the door of the car.

"*You have your bank book,*" said a teller. "*What are you supposed to do here?*"

I told her "*I didn't know,*" and the tellers found a couple checks in my bankbook, wrote out a deposit slip for them, and told me to 'get the devil out of here and go to the hospital.' I laughed it off.

Whatever else I was supposed to do in town that day is erased, and by the time I got home my whole body was starting to ache violently. I was also developing a terrible headache. My wife, Linda, urged me to call the doctor. I laughed it off with the usual:

"*I'm still alive. It can't kill me now.*"

Linda persisted, and by now I was becoming too weak to pick up the phone. I did finally call, however, and I remember the conversation with our family doctor:

"*Hello, Dr. Conaway? This is Bob Milne. Everyone wants me to call you, but I'm just wasting your time.*"

"*Why, Bob? What's wrong?*"

"*Oh, I got hit by lightning. I'm O.K., though.*"

"*WHAT??!! Bob! Did you say 'you got hit by lightning?'*"

"*Yeah, don't worry though. I was in my car. It didn't kill me, so I'll call you tomorrow.*"

"*Bob - wait a minute! Don't hang up! Do you have a headache?*"

"*A headache? Oh, yeah, doc. I got a little headache, but I'll take some aspirins.*"

"*Bob - listen to me! If you don't get in here right now, that headache's going to kill you! Electricity makes all your organs swell up, and your brain swells up, too! Since your brain has nowhere to swell to, if I don't get some cortisone in you fast, YOU'RE GOING TO DIE!*"

"*Oh, yeah? Well, O.K., doc, I'll try and get in there.*"

Before I went to Doc Conaway's, I called the manager in Toledo to tell him I might be late.

"*Late?*" he said. "*Stay home, Bob. Go to the doctor! What the hell's wrong with you? Forget the piano and get someone to take care of you!*"

By the time I did get to Doc Conaway's office, I was barely able to move. Somehow, I had driven myself, made it inside his door, but couldn't make it across the room without crawling. He pumped me full of cortisone, and the headache, arm ache, body ache, and every other kind of excruciating ache that I endured lasted for many days. Also, huge black and blue bruises were appearing on my shoulder and elbow, where I'd been leaning against the door. These were the entrance and exit marks of a tremendous amount of current, I would learn, and they lasted about six weeks before finally disappearing, their aching and throbbing eventually leaving, also. I would also learn about another aspect of electricity: it wipes out memory blocks.

Doc Conaway explained to me that my memory would eventually come back, but it would take possibly six months. The most devastating aspect of memory loss was to short-term memory, and now I couldn't work in my own little sawmill for a while. The guys would come up to me and say, "Hey, Bob - where's the number sixteen spacers for the gang saw?" I would tell them where to find them, but when I turned back to what I was doing I'd find that I'd forgotten that a huge, five-foot sawblade was spinning just two feet in front of me. Therefore, I couldn't do much in the mill for a while.

People seemed to think that lightning won't strike a car, because of the rubber tires. I used to think the same thing, until I found out that lightning is measured in HUNDREDS OF MILLIONS of volts. Thinking logically, it's strong enough to arc between the ground and the clouds. What effect is an insignificant piece of rubber supposed to have on something like that?

I was also told, by several different doctors, that I'd lived because I was in the car. The field went around me, zapping into my shoulder and out my elbow which rested against the door. If my foot had been touching some car frame somehow, it would have gone in my shoulder and out my foot, ripping apart everything it came to the same as it had ripped apart my arm.

I would also find out that I had to relearn how to spell words. I could read them, alright, but I couldn't spell them unless I'd see them in newspapers or books first. Doing crossword puzzles was frustrating, because I'd forget where I put the pencil down every time. I'd forget, in fact, that I even had a pencil at all, and go looking around rooms to find another one while the original sat behind a coffee cup.

I had begun writing novels just previously to this. Now, trying to write was frustrating, because when I'd come to a word that I hadn't seen in the newspaper yet, I couldn't spell it. I remember trying to spell the word 'cry,' unsuccessfully. I tried to reason it out, like they taught me in third grade. I'd pronounce it one letter at a time: Ka - rr - ii. I finally figured out that the letters 'r, y, and c' were involved, and when I couldn't get them in the right order I'd get so frustrated that I'd fling everything in my hands across the room.

Finally, I became awesomely fascinated by lightning. Driving back from Toledo one night, another huge electrical storm came down on me. I pulled to the side of the road, sat in the middle of the car, and studied lightning and the paths it took as much as I could. I actually decided that lightning looked more like it was going up instead of down, because of its forking patterns. Lightning would break off into many forks before it 'hit the ground,' but if we look at a map of a different type of current, the Mississippi River, we see that the forks and branches are running INTO the main stream, not away from it. I wondered if the same were true with this awesome electrical force I was observing as it crashed, forked, rendered and splintered its way across the land again.

Six months eventually went by, and the spelling came back. In the meantime, however, I'd go out to play piano jobs. Someone would say, "Hey, Bob - play 'Georgia Brown.'" Sometimes I'd have to ask them to tell me how it started (like seeing the words in the paper) and then I'd be able to play it again. This was nerve-wracking, because I was in constant fear that someone would decide I was an idiot. I knew the information was in my brain somewhere, but it all had to find its way back to the surface. Another doctor friend of mine, Dr. Bill Winstanley, used to come and sit close to me at piano jobs. When someone would ask me to play something easy, if I couldn't think of how it started, I cast him a quick glance. He'd hum a few bars, to cite an old expression, and I'd be able to pick it up from there.

Today, five years later, I'm past the horrors of this. I no longer worry about what isn't there anymore, because I'm able to find things in my memory anytime I want them. I know there's some holes, though. I have notes that I'd written to myself prior to the strike, and when I look at some of those notes now, I don't have any idea what they referred to.

That's a little scary, but maybe I'm not alone. Ask yourself this question:

"How much have I forgotten in the last year?"

See? There's no way to answer it. The only thing we can do is to look to tomorrow and hope the lightning goes somewhere else next time. I certainly hope it never comes my way again.

OF GREY TAPE AND FLOORBOARDERS

Jack liked the Sundog. It was his favorite watering hole in all of Dearborn in the early seventies. This colorful character was always dressed nattily in a three-piece suit. He stood about five-foot-six and was deceptive in appearance. No one could tell, by first glance, that this man was capable of world-class feats in the art of fast car driving and designing. He was also capable of world-class feats, after a few gins, in the Good-grief-I-don't-believe-it department.

Jack was a brilliant young executive in the design department of a major auto company. He was totally consumed with ingenious ways to make cars work better in every regard. He was also consumed, outside of his job, with making cars go faster than hell. He was an active consultant to a major race car driver, and he also souped up a few buggies for himself. On top of that, he liked to buy foreign cars that were designed for nothing but speed. Some of them resembled the Batmobile.

There was one other thing Jack liked to do. He liked to drink. Jack would quite often sit at the piano bar and relate the latest stories on his pet projects:

"Bob, you won't believe this buggy I'm puttin' together. I can't wait to test it out. Want to go for a ride in a few days?"

"O.K.," I replied, but then Jack added:

"I have to warn you that when we steam this baby up, it'll exert G-forces on you."

"G-forces?" I queried. *"As in..."*

"That's right," he said. *"As in airplanes. The force of acceleration pushes you so far back into the seat you can't move."*

"I'll, uh, let you know," I answered.

Time went on. Other crazy things occurred nightly, and Jack was usually right in the middle of them. One time, on a busy Friday night, I observed him sitting at the bar with drink in hand. An attractive woman came in and was now walking along the bar looking for a place to sit down. The only barstool available was next to, of course, Jack. When she walked on by to see if others were empty further down, I could see Jack starting to cackle to himself. He knew she would have to eventually sit next to him. I knew what would happen when she did.

Of course, the lady finally came back. She set her purse on the bar as she sat down. Elmer, the bartender, looked first at me, then to the ceiling in anticipation of what we all knew was going to happen, and then went to take her order. Jack, somewhat ruddied from gin, was smirking.

The place was busy. I was playing requests for people around the piano and trying to simultaneously watch the bar. The lady was sitting comfortably so far, and Jack hadn't even said a word to her. So far, so good.

"Reservation for Jones, party of three!"

People were getting up to go to their tables as I worked through the 'Yellow Dog Blues,' and as I noticed Jack lean over to say something to her. She smiled politely, then tried to ignore him.

"Hey, Bob; play some country-western."

"I don't play any country-western. I only play hillbilly."

It was a stock answer intended for fun, but now Jack was mumbling something else to her. Elmer turned away so he wouldn't be caught in the middle when it hit the fan.

"Have I told you lately that I love you..."

Someone was singing along with the tune. I had a cup of coffee on the piano, and some woman leaned over and stuffed two dollars in, thinking it was a tip glass. I smiled and thanked her. Don't embarrass the customers. Uh-oh. The woman at the bar just turned her back to Jack, who was cackling and laughing to himself. She didn't look too happy about something either, and was straining to see if any other barstools had opened up. They hadn't.

"Hi, Bob. How ya' doing?"

Some customers were sitting down at the piano. I recognized the man but hadn't seen any of the others.

"Bob, I'd like you to meet my wife and daughter..."

"Hi. How are you?" I smiled. In the background, Jack was grinning fiendishly as he now leaned over the woman's shoulder to whisper something in her ear. But I was trying to pay attention to the people in front of me:

"My husband has told me about this place. It's really quite nice," replied this guy's wife as they all sat down. Then, from the bar:

"OH MY GOD! YOU'RE DISGUSTING!" followed by:

"Bartender! Can you do anything to shut this guy up?"

I looked up to see Jack cackling, and I knew exactly what he'd done. He had certain stock phrases for 'breaking the ice' with lovely young ladies, and there was no doubt as to which phrase he'd just used. Trust me, it can't be printed.

Poor Elmer, trying to somehow assuage the situation, laughed as he answered the lady:

"Sure," he replied. *"We can shut up Jack. I've got just the stuff."*

Elmer produced a roll of grey tape that had been left by some furnace workers. Three inches wide, he tore off a piece about a foot long, walked up to Jack, and plastered it over his mouth. The journeyman, dumbstruck, tried to somehow manage to listen as the guy in front of me, unaware of the horror show going on in back of him, proudly explained:

"My daughter here is taking piano lessons. She's doing very well."

I tried to look at the daughter and say something appropriate, but behind them was Jack, sitting on a barstool with his mouth grey-taped shut. He was just shaking in drunken glee.

"I'm, uh, happy to hear that," I answered politely to the daughter, as the woman at the bar, half sitting on the stool and half standing on the floor, turned to Jack. I could hear her raise her voice to say to him:

"There, you dirty-mouthed little smart-ass. What are ya' going to do now?"

Without a second's hesitation, Jack fell off his barstool, ending up sitting on the floor with his back to the bar. The woman looked down with a satisfied smirk, but she wouldn't be smirking long. Now Jack came up off the floor under her straight skirt. When his head hit her crotch, she went straight up off the stool and landed four-square on the barroom floor. With a horrifying shriek, she got up, grabbed her purse, and went flying out the door. Jack, grey-taped, was still on the floor, leaning back against the bar. He was shaking violently from his own cackling, and the speechless journeyman tried to listen to the proud parent still telling about his daughter:

"She's got all the scales and arpeggios down. She thinks she'd like to be in this business someday..."

About a month later I heard the story from the police department. They'd bought a new radar unit and took it out to the expressway one night to try it out. I knew that Jack had just finished building the car he'd been telling me about, and now it came to light that as the police tested their new unit, they immediately realized something was wrong with it. The first blip that came down the throughway registered 140 miles an hour. They reset the dials and started over.

But further down the throughway, another cop saw something go by like a bat out of hell. Unable to get anywhere near it, he radioed ahead for a road block. Eventually, Jack showed up at the road block, driving at the speed limit. Not the least bit drunk, he tipped his hat to the gentlemen and drove through.

It seems that one of the prerequisites for being a journeyman is being able to hold a whole bunch of information inside, and never - NEVER - tell where it came from. Scales and arpeggios, indeed!

WHAT A WAY TO GO

Dave was a good guy. Everyone liked him. He was congenial, funny, and very intelligent. He was one of those mid-fifty-ish, Hemingway-bearded guys that would hang around in blue jeans and flannel shirts all day and all night in the riverfront saloon where the Sweet Violets played, and no one would ever know that he was a highly respected college professor. I guess you could say that Dave was earthy, but in the true sense of the word. He didn't try to assume airs.

Dave had a girl-friend. Pam was extremely good looking, a school teacher, and just as intelligent as he was. The only difference between them, and everyone commented on it, was her age. She was at least twenty-five years younger than he. But this is not for us to pass judgment on, for love doesn't recognize age differences. Love just exists, like it did for Dave and Pam.

Pam's mother came into the saloon one night, and her entrance was noticed by everyone. Sally was early fifty-ish, recently divorced, blond, stacked, and otherwise built like a brick bath house, and she did nothing to conceal her natural endowments. She was very pleasant, intelligent, also a school teacher, and very approving of her daughter's relationship with Dave. Sometimes the three of them sat together for whole evenings and listened to the band.

Dave eventually retired from teaching college, and we all knew what his retirement plans were. He had bought a sailboat and planned to sail around the world with Pam. It sounded like a dream, and we all learned of the plans over the ensuing months. They would head out into the Atlantic ocean, sail north up the coast to Nova Scotia, then head for - who knows where? Incredible. And money was no problem. They were just plain going to get on the boat and sail for the next year or two, however long it took them to accomplish the deed.

Sally was excited about the trip also and now, over the months preceeding the departure, we noticed the three of them together on an increasing basis. Wherever was one, were three.

They huddled over the tables in the saloon with maps and charts. They could be seen in a car running around doing errands, and finally we got the news: Sally was going on the trip also. She had quit her job as a teacher, as had Pam, and the two stunning ladies - mother and daughter - were prepared to crawl into the galley with the good professor and go galley-west. When Dave first informed me of this,

I had never seen such a, uh, bath-eating grin on anyone's face. Hmm...

Then they were off, and everyone who was aware of this entourage imagined the same thing as the boat rode up and down among the waves, up and down between crests and valleys. Grown men with true grit were seen to bite their tongues and lips to keep from making comments as the boat rode up and down upon the waves, up and down between the crests and valleys.

We received periodic postcards from the trio. They'd read something like:

"Hi guys! Having a blast! Wish you were here, 'har har!'"

We'd choke, look at each other silently, then try to play a tune and forget what we'd seen. But then, after two months at sea, or at whatever, we received a card that gave us concern. Dave had suffered a heart attack off the coast of England and had undergone surgery. The card was quick to add, however, that the ladies anxiously awaited his return to the decks below so they could pick up where they left off and continue the journey. I don't know what was so interesting about the ceiling of the saloon that night, but everyone who read the card just sat there looking upward for a moment before passing it on.

Eventually, after about a year and a half, we received word that they'd returned. Sure enough, the trio came into the saloon one night filled with tales of the trip. During a break, I happened to bump into Dave as he was picking up some drinks at the bar:

"How was the trip?" I asked.

"Excellent!" he roared. *"Couldn't have been better!"*

"Well," I ventured, *"how are you feeling following the heart attack?"*

Dave chuckled to himself at the memory of it, then replied with a grin:

"I have never felt better in my life, Bob. Never felt better in my life!"

As he stood beaming next to me, I looked over to the two gorgeous women waiting for him at the table. They were talking non-stop to some people about the trip, and this whole thing resembled a scene from some surrealistic, pipe-dreamish movie, but it wasn't. Finally, and with great courage, I managed to say:

"Uh, Dave, I don't know how to say this, but it seems that a great many men could have become easily confused in that boat out there."

With a roar of laughter, he replied:

"I understand, Bob. I understand! Whaa-haa!"

And with that, he gathered up the drinks for the trio, strode back to the table, toasted the traditional Spanish *'Salud!'* and they drank.

But there's more. Soon we were to learn that the trio had moved into Dave's house, a short distance from the saloon. And now we'd never see just one of them alone, for the three were inseparable. They were always laughing, friendly, willing to talk about the trip, and naturally evasive about any suggestion as to what everyone knew existed. But who cared? It seemed like most people were quiet and approving, not pompous and condemning. Dave and the ladies were happy, which was enough to make anyone envious.

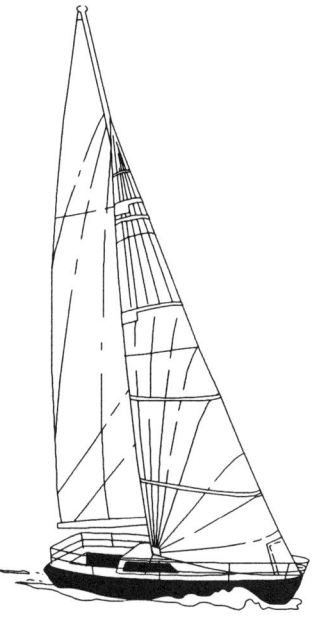

Then came tragedy. Dave's heart was unable to keep up with whatever level of activity his body was putting out, and this time the heart attack meant the end. A small funeral was attended by those who knew him, and his two special friends were greatly distraught over the circumstances. The ladies disappeared soon after, never to be seen again. We heard rumors that they'd gone to Mexico, but nobody knew for sure. The three of them were now simply gone, leaving us with nothing but memories of their boundless spirits, their unbelievable trip and, of course, their bizarre life style.

In the years that followed, whenever the topic of Dave came up one comment was always sure to be heard. It was always meant as a compliment because it WAS a compliment, and also because we all loved Dave and his two friends. Someone would raise a glass for a moment of silence and remembrance, then say with the deepest of respect:

'Salud, brothers! What a way to go!'

HOW ARE YOU TODAY, SIR?

The professional piano player develops a 'sixth sense' about customers. This is a necessity, not a quirk, because it helps to know ahead of time what kind of reaction someone is likely to give you.

One time, many years ago, I remember playing in a fashionable hotel lounge as people came and went through a doorway about sixty feet to my right. Therefore, if I happened to be looking straight ahead, it was peripheral vision that told me when someone came in the door. Peripheral vision almost always correctly told me whether it was a man or woman coming in, regardless of how they were dressed. This always puzzled me, because even if a woman was wearing jeans, a shirt, and had short hair, I immediately knew which gender she was as soon as she entered the furthest outskirts of my vision. I was wrong occasionally, of course, but not very often.

After years of trusting peripheral vision as to genders, I remember one time when a man came and sat down at the piano with me. Every instinct I had told me not to attempt conversation with this guy, so I looked at him to try to figure out what caused me to think in such a way. He was nicely dressed, looked calm enough, and didn't in the least way appear to have been inebriated, so I finally (totally going against my own grain) ventured a comment:

"Hello, sir. How are you today?"

His eyes flashed as he looked toward me, then snapped: *"What is this? I come in here for a quiet drink and I have to talk to you?"*

This launched my own personal study as to why peripheral vision tipped me off to attitudes as well. I would come to learn that I was close to 100% right, long before the person in question ever sat down near me. I found that, without looking up from the keys, I was wanting the person who just came through the door to sit at the piano with me, or that I was hoping with everything in me that he'd sit somewhere else. After years of trying to figure out why this was, I finally related it to another study that I do.

Animals, I find, are incredible. They possess senses that go way beyond what we understand. A common example is when a dog knows if you are afraid of it or not. If the dog senses you are afraid, it bolsters its drive to attack. If it senses you are not afraid, it will back off.

This ability, I wondered, might be a repressed sense that we humans have. Is it a smell, a walk, a gait, the way someone holds their head, or what? Whatever it is, I found that I had picked up on it and, as previously stated, I was close to 100% right. Also, it came to me through peripheral vision, not a detailed study of the person. It also caused me to develop a rather severe attitude: trust my initial impression; don't ever doubt what you already know is true.

This does not mean that if I avoided someone once I will always avoid them, for the next time the person comes through the door he might be walking differently, or whatever.

I have always been fascinated by an animal's ability to know what's going to happen before it happens. For instance, burrowing animals such as rabbits, moles, and even field rats and mice can tell when a flood is coming a day or two before it hits. Therefore, they get out of the valley and onto the high ground before they're trapped down their holes, or wake up to find they're on an island that will be underwater shortly.

So I've wondered if we still possess the same innate abilities, but that they've been shuttled out of our 'civilized' existence. I think we do. I think we hear it referred to as 'vibes.' Someone has 'good vibes,' or this place has 'bad vibes.' If so, then maybe it's 'vibes' that tell me, when I'm sitting at a piano somewhere, to avoid some character at all costs. Maybe it's 'vibes' that tell me that the guy looking at me is going to open his mouth and say 'play it again, Sam.' Maybe it's 'vibes' that tell me to say, when someone is explaining a business deal away from the piano, *"I'll think about it and call you,"* then never call back and stay away from the phone for a week.

It is about 7:00. One more hour of playing cocktail piano before I can go home. But the lounge is kind of cheerful today. Can you see all the nicely dressed people having a good time over by the bar? The guy and gal over at the hors d'oeuvres table are in a friendly mood, too. I don't even have to look too closely to know that. It's days like this that make this job enjoyable.

Look; if I put a little trill on this note, those two at the table will look over here and laugh. It's that kind of day. I'll hit this minor chord in 'The Entertainer,' and the guy at the hors d'oeuvres table will turn with a silly smirk on his face. If I...

Oh, God; did you see what just walked in the door? No, I don't know his name and I haven't turned to look at him yet. I don't even know the color of his suit. In fact, I don't know anything at all about this guy, except that I know as much, if not more, than I need to know about him right now.

A STREET FROM TIME

circa 1972

Empty sidewalk, beside the riverfront
Lost in the shadow left by time passing by,
Skidrow beerhall, with boards on windows,
Can you imagine there is love in this cold,
In this old empty sidewalk I call home?

Well, if you...
See in the sidewalk, a hundred gone faces
From an age when they danced,
When they sang out in glory,
When they rode with the circus,
When they laughed with the clown,
When they cried, not ashamed,
When their glory rode down,
Then you'll see in the lamplight
My one hundred brothers
One and all.

Oh, see how he dances, with the joy of a kitten
How they watch and grow spellbound
As the wind plays his rhythm
How he floats through the doorways
Of a forgotten hall,
How he turns on a nickel
How they cry, when he falls,
How his hand holds the whiskey,
Can you see in the lamplight
One and all?

Hear the wind blow! Through hollow doorways
Rocking this cradle with the
lullaby called 'Time',
And droning foghorns, across the river
Sound like they sing you of the
Symphony of strife, the finale to
the rhapsody of life...

So if you...
See, on the sidewalk,
A broken man sitting
With his face to the heavens
I can tell you he's thinking
Of the sound of his music
When he played 'cross the land,
And the legions of voices
That sang works of his hand,
And of choirs of angels
To sing through the lamplight
Once and all

So, tell me a story
Make me smile once again
For the heyday has vanished
And the stagelights have dimmed,
Let them dance on the sidewalk
Let them smile to the sky,
In the night wings a memory
In the 'morrow we die,
And will you look in the lamplight
At my one hundred brothers -
One and all?

Empty sidewalk, beside the riverfront
Photo by Richard Berry, 1992

THE TIMES THEY ARE A' CHANGIN'

We all have a tendency to look out the window and see the birds, trees, or anything else that appears to us and not really realize that the birds we're seeing are generations removed from the birds we saw when we were younger. The old ones have died off many times over, but we're still here. The following is a small compendium of events that have signaled to the Journeyman Piano Player that he ain't as young as he used to be. Perhaps these incidents will remind you of similar ones in your life.

ACT ONE: I am playing the piano at the Rathskeller when an attractive, 30-year-old female sits down on the piano bench with me:

30 y.o.: *"Hi Bob."*
Bob: *"Hi."*
30 y.o.: *"I really like your piano playing."*
Bob: *"Thank you."*
30 y.o.: *"I've always wanted to play like you."*
Bob: *"How nice of you to say that."*
30 y.o.: *"Yes. Many years ago, when I was a real little girl, my mother took me to a record store and bought me one of your records. Wow; that was EONS ago!"*

I didn't react. I just continued playing the piano. I didn't even feel a twinge. Not a one. I just smiled and nodded to her, 'cause I'd have cried if I'd tried to talk.

ACT TWO; Scene one: The Journeyman Piano Player is playing at a fancy place in West Bloomfield when someone he doesn't even recognize (S.D.R. for short) walks up bringing the following conversation with him:

S.D.R.: *"Hi Bob. I haven't seen you in ten years."*
Bob: *"Hi. It's nice to see you."*
S.D.R.: *"Wow, Bob. Have you ever gained weight!"*

ACT TWO; Scene two: Same place, different night. This time, a man and woman approach. They are smirking. The man pulls out a photograph of three musicians on a stage somewhere or other and shows it. While I'm playing the piano, the woman asks,

"Do you recognize these guys?"

After squinting uselessly, they finally figure out that I can't even make out the forms without my glasses. As hubby holds the picture, the woman pulls glasses out of my pocket and puts them on me. After a brief moment, I reply:

"Who are those guys?"

They giggle. They smirk. Finally she says:

"That's - YOU! Playing at our wedding twenty-one years ago!"

I didn't have the foggiest idea what to say.

ACT THREE: At Nancy Whiskey's Barroom Joint, sometime last summer. The Sweet Violets Ragtime Band has been playing New Orleans jazz and is now taking a short break.

Chuck Moss, the great trombonist from Rochester, Michigan, and the Journeyman Piano Player are sitting at the bar. I am bemoaning the fact that a slight wrist paralysis bothers me. Moss offers the use of some of his vitamin B pills, citing great meritorious feats that he knows them to be capable of. I wonder aloud if they would help against a gout affliction. Moss offers evidence in the affirmative, based on personal experience. Suddenly, Moss and the journeyman look at each other kind of strangely, for these same two characters used to terrorize bars of all descriptions some twenty years ago around Rochester. After a moment of silence, I offered the following observation:

"Moss; do you realize that we have just sat here for twenty minutes talking about pills?"

After another brief pause in which Moss looked at the ceiling first, the walls next, the beautiful ladies sitting all over the place that we hadn't once mentioned, and the rows upon rows of booze and beer sitting behind the bar, he replied, as if annoyed:

"I really wish you hadn't said that."

IT'S BEEN A LONG, LONG TIME...

The true Journeyman Piano Player has to wear many hats. During the piano heyday of the seventies and early eighties, I was playing anywhere from fourteen to twenty engagements per week. Every style imaginable was required, including easy listening, country-western, ragtime, show tunes, and on down the list. Two gigs a day was standard, and a third and sometimes fourth was not unusual.

Consider the following schedule:
Monday through Friday:
    5:00 to 8:00 at a fancy hotel piano bar.
    8:30 to 11:00 at a local seafood house.
Saturday:
    7:30 to 8:30; solo piano at a riverfront saloon.
    9:00 to 1:30; with the Sweet Violets Ragtime
    Band at the same saloon.
Sunday:
    7:00 to 11:00 at the seafood house.

Add to this the fact that I played lunch gigs quite often. Two summers were spent playing from noon to 2:00 on riverboat lunch cruises in Toledo, some sixty miles south of the above schedule.

This was the standard schedule that went week-in and week-out for about eight years. Both before and after those eight years consisted of the same number of hours, but in different places. Mix into this frequent television or radio morning shows, yacht and country clubs, band dates, and agents calling up with some strange job. One time I got paid with an airline ticket for two, anyplace in the country, anytime I wanted to go.

A young pianist, not too long ago, fretted over playing his first job in public. At the end of his first set he sighed to me:

"Gee, Mr. Milne, what a relief. That was my first set."

When I told him he'd done pretty good for the first one, he looked up and asked:

"Just out of curiosity, how many sets do you think you've played?"

I did a little double-take when he asked that, and thought about the question considerably as he played his second set. I used the proverbial bar napkin on which to do some scribbling:

'Let's see - how many years did I play two jobs a day? That's six to eight sets a day, six or seven days a week. Saturday nights alone used to be 7-1/2 hours for almost ten years. Now, how many years of four sets a day? Five sets? The Sundog alone was a five-hour job six nights a week for how many years? Three? Four? And when did this whole thing start? Was it 1964? 1962? How many sets a week do I play now? Should I count radio shows? Recording sessions? Nah, probably not. Hmm, I should probably use the approximate number of hours I played per week, multiply that times the number of years...what else is there...how close can I actually come with this...?

About half an hour later, he looked up and inquired:
"Well?"
It was with great difficulty that I replied:
"About thirty-three thousand."

The answer made me cringe; **THIRTY-THREE THOUSAND SETS?**

Why, I can remember the first one as clearly as if I played it last week, even though it was over thirty years ago. It was at the Treadway Inn, Rochester, New York, when I was a French horn major at the Eastman School of Music. But - **thirty-three thousand?**

How long ago was this when I played horn in the Rochester Philharmonic, hurled fast-pitch softball and played on college basketball teams? One of my good friends was Bob Zimmerman, fantastic string bass player and son of Oscar Zimmerman, who played principal bass with Toscanini. Bob and I went places, played on basketball leagues, had fun, and - **thirty-three thousand sets?**

The Treadway had a Gay Nineties night every weekend. They'd throw checkered tablecloths over the lunch-room tables, wheel an old upright piano in from the hallway, and serve pitchers of beer to college students as someone played sing-a-long tunes on the piano. Irving Crane, the legendary U.S. pool-playing champion would often come in after his day job across the street. The phenomenal artistry of this man could easily fill many books, and since pool fascinates me he was a reigning hero to this awe-struck little college student. Lessons I learned from Crane allowed me, many years later, to play an exhibition match against another man whose name is still mentioned around pool rooms, Willie Mosconi.

I used to go to the Treadway with fellow students to possibly talk with Crane and for the sheer fun of being there, and one night we found they had no piano player. I could play rudimentary enough piano to fill in for him, learning new tunes from someone singing to me. But then Mikhail, the Ukranian manager, offered me a job on the weekends. It paid ten dollars a night and all the beer you could drink.

They'd take the front off the piano to let the sound out, and people would stand around hoisting their mugs as they sang all the favorites from the twenties and thirties; songs that were as old then as Elvis and the Beatles are now.

"Please Don't Talk About Me When I'm Gone..."

The piano was never in tune, and I learned that hitting the melody notes slightly ahead of the bass notes made it easier for the listener to follow. The piano's overall muddiness was overcome by this method, and when I eventually heard ragtime syncopated on pianos which were in tune, it made me wonder if out-of-tune pianos might have had something to do with the birth of the style.

I would learn, years later, that my harmonies to many of these sing-a-long tunes would have to be changed slightly to play with bands. In the Treadway, I harmonized everything I heard in accordance with a choice of pleasing chords available. Many of the tunes I had never heard performed by anyone at all. I had been forced, in fact, to compose my own harmonies to go along with the guys singing the songs. If I didn't do this, there would be no job and consequently no twenty bucks each weekend for a poor student who desperately needed it. When I would by chance hear a familiar tune on the radio or in a club, I would pay attention to the harmonies to see how close my arrangements were.

Mikhail told me that the job went from eight o'clock to one o'clock, no breaks. Since I didn't know any better, I played it as he said until, as months went by, I realized that this wasn't right. The customers helped me come up with a plan. All the guys would huddle around the piano singing loudly, then one of us would take a beer and throw it across the felt hammers. This would cause the entire action to perform sluggishly; the keys wouldn't come back up.

"Mikhail! Mikhail! Some drunk spilled a beer into the piano! The keys won't work!"

"Mmm," he'd mumble. *"You hat best let eet dry out, mein sohn."*

"Darn," I'd say straight-away. With practice, we discovered that by arcing the beer just right, we were able to decommission the piano for forty-five minutes before the keys worked again.

Thirty-three thousand sets? My little pocket computer tells me this equals - oh, never mind. But it also takes me back to the piano at the Peabody Book Store, in Baltimore, Maryland. It was the summer of 1964, and I was playing horn in the Baltimore Symphony summer season.

After four years of Eastman, I went to the Peabody Institute in Baltimore for a year. The Peabody Book Store, only a few blocks away, had nothing at all to do with the school, but was rather a prohibition-era gimmick designed to hide a speak-easy. The bookstore was underneath a brownstone apartment building. You walk down three or four steps to get in, and then browse through stacks of antique books while some little bespectacled character sits behind his desk watching you. When you come to the back of the store, you see a passageway between some shelves and Voila! - you emerge into this genuine 1920's speak-easy, complete with piano.

I played this piano during the summer of 1964. The job payed the usual ten bucks, or fifteen if they had a good night. Although the owner, a woman named Rose, had no problem with my taking a break from time to time, the piano itself had drawbacks; many of the keys barely worked. It was during this time that I learned to play all the tunes on the notes that did work, the black keys. It seemed that the previous flailers of the instrument had confined their flailings to the standard keys of C, F, and G, so now the apprentice Journeyman learned to either play on the notes that worked or look for another job.

I remember one incident in which a customer ordered some crab cakes, a Baltimore (pronounced Ba'muh by the locals) specialty. After a wait of about half an hour, he asked the waiter where his crab cakes were.

"*Oh,*" replied the waiter. "*Did you order the crab cakes? Well, they looked so good, the cook ate them himself.*"

Thirty-three thousand, eh?

But I can still see the thick wooden tables, Rose's face, and the sight of the cook gulping down the crab cakes behind the bar.

"*The cook ate 'em?*" yelled the indignant customer, not at all amused. "*Well then, tell him to make some more!*"

Can this be??? **Thirty-three thousand?**

How long ago was this when I watched Irving Crane, in a game of straight pool, intentionally leave himself a ninety-degree angle on the break shot. Then he stroked it in so thin that the ball barely made it to the pocket as the other balls exploded all over the table from the

177

force of the blast. What a sight, and he made it look so easy! What a magnificent sight! And it was the nine-ball that rolled so slowly through it all.

Then I went over to the Treadway to stroke the keys. What if I tried to make it look easy, like he did? Is there some key to performance that's locked in appearance? Come to think of it, that's what I always tried to do with the horn. I'd stand in front of a mirror for hours in the orchestra room under the stage of the Eastman Theatre, watching myself play horn and trying to make it look as simple as possible. Do I dare try to learn - a piano this way...?

Thirty-three thousand?

I can still smell the musty books and see the bespectacled little man in among them all. I can still hear Mikhail's heavy accent cutting through the English language at the Treadway Inn, and I can hear the crab cakes sizzling and taste their seasoning, hanging thick as the northern lights in the air of the Peabody Book Store.

I can still hear - yea, feel - the Rochester Philharmonic winding into the thundering finale of Johannes Brahms' second symphony (the horns are holding that screaming high note that brings in the echo chorus!) and I'm running around on the basketball court with Bob Zimmerman again. I just made a hook shot from thirty feet out, but now the conductor's tapping his baton. He wants the Mozart piano concerto and Verne Reynolds is signaling me to pull it out of the folder...

"Come on, kid; play me another set. And another one after that. You remind me of something, I don't know what, but you remind me of something that happened - just yesterday."

END